FRIENDS IN FAITH

To Anna,
With much gratitude
for your friendship, ministry,
and encouragement.

Carl

19 January 1997

FRIENDS IN FAITH

An Episcopal Priest Speaks
to the Questions of Our Time

✝

Carl R. Hansen

Volume 1

SUNFLOWER INK PUBLISHING

37931 Palo Colorado Road, Carmel, California 93923

(paperback) 9 8 7 6 5 4 3 2 1

FRIENDS IN FAITH

Library of Congress Catalogue Card No. 96-071330
ISBN 0-931104-44-0

TABLE OF CONTENTS

PREFACE

The woman's voice cracked with emotion on the other end of the phone as she described her pain. She and her husband had raised her now divorced daughter in an evangelical Christian home with traditional values and immersion in their church community. Although a Christian, the daughter's ex-husband had been domineering and abusive. The family was devastated by the divorce, no one more so than the daughter, who struggled for years with the contradiction between the commitment she had made and the struggle for her own identity.

Now, the daughter has met a wonderful man whom she has been dating for some time and they wish to be married. He is nurturing and thoughtful, prays with the family at meals, and from all appearances, is deeply in love with their daughter. Is there rejoicing in this household? Is there a great sense of God's blessing and renewal upon this family, now that the daughter has survived one of life's ordeals and entered into a glimpse of the Promised Land? On the contrary, the emotional trauma of the mother was as though her daughter had just been diagnosed with cancer.

You see, the prospective groom is not a professing Christian by the standards of the family's church, so the pastor will not marry the hopeful and otherwise happy couple. It does not matter that he manifests the fruits of the Spirit. He has not said the magical words and crossed the doctrinal line. He is deemed unworthy to stand in the presence of "true believers," many who probably cannot hold a candle to him from the standard of the love of Christ. This mother is suffering from the abuse of Christians who teach that the only true marriages are marriages where both parties are Christian by their own definition.

Let me introduce you to another sufferer of such abuse. John came to a workshop entitled, "The Church and Homosexuality." Most of the twenty or so people who signed up were gay. John was in his 70's. The first session began with the standard "Why I'm here" exercise. I'll never forget John's response. It wasn't what he said so much as the depth of his pain after so many years which moved me. John is Roman Catholic. He loves the Church with every cell of his body. But it is unrequited love. For over 70 years the passion he holds for the Body of Christ has been spurned when he ventured to trust and to seek the resources of the church in his search for spiritual wholeness. John sobbed as he released his pain in a safe environment.

Then there is Sam, a middle-aged, spiritual man who was raised in a strict fundamentalist home. His father was an itinerant missionary as he grew up, and Sam learned very early that evil abounds not only in the world, but in the soul, and that he must be vigilant against that enemy which lurks in everyone not like his own kind and disguises itself in anything which smacks of pleasure. Thankfully, Sam grew to reject that way of thinking, but in the process unconsciously rejected a personal relationship with Jesus Christ. Jesus is associated in his subconscious with the spiritual abuse of his childhood. He is now a devotee of many spiritual experiences and perspectives, but a child of none. He is trying to find the Jesus he knew as a child, but the churches he encounters still speak the language of the abuse he knows all too well.

These are real stories drawn from some of my more recent experiences in ministry. I doubt that you, the reader, will be surprised to read about them. While statistics show that a large majority of people are believers in God, and many are faithful churchgoers, there is an uneasy sense that the church no longer speaks our language. The categorical statements of doctrine, as they have been divisively applied over the centuries, no longer resonate with the Holy Spirit speaking to the soul of modern believers.

There are some, of course, who doggedly hang on to the past. In reaction to the efforts of others to keep pace with the work of the Spirit in the world and in our churches and synagogues, they fearfully condemn what they perceive as a liberal agenda of relativism and "modernism." These folks seem to interpret tradition as the Holy Spirit pulling us from behind rather than leading us forward into the future. They continue to define their particular tradition as a fortress against the world and the sole container of God's truth. Their ethical elixir is to universally apply selected passages of the Bible as a book of legalisms. They, like the Pharisees whom Jesus confronted, view themselves as faithful to God, the remnant in a world gone corrupt and out of favor with God.

This book is not for them; it is for Sam, John, and the family whom I mentioned above. It is for those who are the outcasts, the abandoned, the poor in spirit. It is for those who long for the nurture of a loving faith community, but are made to feel unacceptable by the churches they know and hear about. And it is for those who may not feel the longing, but whose faith may be sparked by this book. Most of all, this book is for my Lord, Jesus. I pray that it will serve and please him, that it is inspired by him alone, and that it will further the work of his kingdom in its readers.

In Acts 2:11, people from many regions and cultures were gathered in Jerusalem as pilgrims for the Feast of Pentecost when the Holy Spirit descended upon the apostles and they spoke in the many varied languages of the people assembled. They were amazed as they related, "In our own languages we hear them speaking about God's deeds of power." It is my hope that what is contained herein will speak the language of God's love to the reader, wherever he or she is on the spiritual pilgrimage. God came to love us personally in Jesus Christ, and the Holy Spirit is continuing in us what God did in Jesus for all - seeking us out, inviting us into intimacy, and enlivening us with faith and power. My prayer is that this book speaks your language.

The book is a collection of columns I have written over the past few years for the Monterey County Herald and Scripps-Howard News Service. One could call me a theological Ann Landers. From the questions submitted to me there has developed an articulation of the Good News which is not my creation alone. It is my inheritance as a priest in The Episcopal Church, and through my church a gift from God as revealed in the Judeo-Christian tradition. The arrangement of the columns in this book is under seven general themes, yet any given column may speak to several themes in the course of my response. A column addressing a social issue, for example, may contain a considerable amount of biblical teaching. To this extent, the columns are arranged somewhat arbitrarily.

The views contained herein did not come to me in an ecstatic vision such as St. John had on Patmos. They are the fruit of many loving influences over a lifetime, deep struggles, times of error and soul searching, feeble efforts to maintain a vital devotional life, and a fairly typical lifestyle as a father, husband, businessman, and in my later years, priest.

If anything I have written is out of step with Christ, I trust the Lord to make corrections in the thoughts of the reader - and mine. I have been asked to respond to mysteries for which I am little prepared, despite seminary, eighteen years of priesthood, and fifty-three years of life. I have done my best to proclaim what has been given to me, and I will continue to proclaim it joyfully in the conviction that what gives my life power and meaning is intended to be shared.

I thank God for all who have helped me over the years to articulate the faith through these columns. I am especially grateful to Linda Dowd who has faithfully proofread and commented upon my writing. To Perry Walker, who, as friend and senior warden of All Saints shared and reinforced the vision of this evangelistic effort. And to Alan McEwen, who helped enormously to get the column ready for Scripps-Howard News Service. All Saints Parish, whom I have been privileged to serve for almost nine years, has provided the "space" for me to venture into this expression of the Gospel. And I must also thank individual members of the parish and the many readers across the country who have encouraged me by responding to the column with their appreciation, questions and comments. I include those who have taken the time to express their disagreement. They are an important part of the ongoing process of formation which I consider a blessing from God.

Without the confidence placed in me by Susan Miller, publisher and editor of the Monterey County Herald, this book would not exist. I am thankful for her support, and trust the weekly column has served the newspaper and its readers well. I am also grateful to Scripps-Howard News Service for valuing the column and distributing "Friends in Faith" nationally and releasing the copyright so that this book could be published.

For the cover art, I am grateful to cartoonist Eldon Dedini, a parishioner of All Saints Parish. The joyous procession on Carmel Beach, with symbols of Monterey Bay and the All Saints banner, is a fitting impression for a book created in the midst of a loving faith community. The cartoon was created for All Saints' 75th Anniversary in 1987, and I am grateful to the parish for allowing me to share it with readers.

Finally, I thank my family. Their presence in my life provides both affirmation and challenge. My wife, Susan, my children John and Julie, and my step-children Justin, Joe, Alaina, and Nick, have each lifted me up in their own way while keeping my feet firmly on the ground of life's joys, struggles and changes.

PRAYER

PRAYER

Would you say something about prayer? I try to pray, but sometimes I give up because it seems like God doesn't answer me.

Dryness in prayer is very common among people of faith. Even those who have a rich prayer life will go through such periods. Don't be too discouraged when it happens. It's part of a healthy relationship with God.

On the other hand, if you never experience meaningful prayer, there are some things you can do to increase your ability to hear God. Here are some suggestions.

Set aside time to pray. Prayer is simply spending intentional time with God. By designating "space" for your fellowship with God, and in making sacred time and place in the course of your day, your practice of prayer becomes an offering. The sacrifice is that you give up for God whatever else you might have done with that space in your day.

At first, you might find it difficult to find the time to slow down and enter your sacred place, but soon you will discover that it is the most important part of your day. Setting apart space for God is the most significant thing you can do to experience God's presence. Jesus made sure that he made such spaces in his life, despite people constantly pressing their own needs upon him.

Of course, you do not have to pray only in that prayer space. Prayer can be unceasing, as St. Paul says. But the sacred place grounds the rest of your day in the Spirit of God and you will find yourself becoming part of that long tradition of saints whose lives become increasingly whole simply because they take the time to let God work in them.

Trust that God always answers. Try not to judge what an answer to prayer is. Be open to whatever the answer is, even the appearance of no answer at all. We'd like to get some clear direction, but answers through prayer often take time. God's wisdom in love supports us in our struggles without making it too easy for us. Sometimes it seems as though the answers aren't as important as the benefit we receive from standing in God's presence through sincere and earnest prayer.

We can trust that God knows our every need. We know that God's perspective is much greater than our own. Sometimes we receive exactly what we want. Sometimes it seems we get what we don't want. Sometimes it seems there is no answer at all. Yet, prayer is not like catching those little floating yellow ducklings hoping to get the one with the prize on the bottom. With God, every prayer is a big winner, although the nature of the prize may take some time to be revealed.

Christian prayer, in particular, is not simply asking God for what we want. As we pray, we also trust God to give what is best for us. Sometimes it feels as though God must be cruel or indifferent. But when we stay with our prayers, we will begin to experience unfolding grace, no matter what the situation may be. Often our prayer gives us a new level of trust, a new perspective, a call to action, or simply the ability to be patient. These are supreme blessings.

Listen more, speak less. There is nothing so rewarding in prayer as the quieting of the mind in order to allow God to heal and renew us. Many techniques are available to you in the practice of prayerful meditation, contemplation, and listening prayer. Many people feel that God doesn't answer because they have not developed the art of listening to God. Talk to your spiritual leader or a good friend who has a vital prayer life, and you will surely learn some of the ways you, too, can be more receptive to the movement of God within you.

PRAYER

*For many months I've been
praying for the same list of people over and over and
I've been feeling burned out. Is there any way to pray
without feeling burned out? How can I be sure that
God answers prayers?*

I t is common to feel frustrated in prayer. You have been praying
with no apparent answers, and naturally wonder if God is listening.

It requires a certain amount of faith to pray at all. We believe in the existence of God, albeit with some doubts, perhaps. We also have a natural concern for people in need, especially loved ones. Belief in God together with concern for others brings us to prayer. But this is only the beginning.

The frustration you feel is God's way of inviting you to deepen your faith. Belief in God is more than the intellectual acceptance of God's existence and goodness. That something more is best described as trust. To believe in God is to give our concerns to God in prayer. When you pray for people, think of yourself as releasing them. You are acknowledging that they are already in God's hands, so you can pray for them with a profound sense of peace and trust. Your feelings of burnout are symptomatic of thinking that your prayers are responsible for the welfare of others. When this thinking is carried to an extreme, we can torture ourselves with fear that we are not praying rightly or with enough frequency. We can also be abused by charlatans who allege success in prayer and are seeking our "donations." We need to remember that prayer is not a matter of technique or of human gifts. Rather, it is trusting the heart of God.

Because prayer is based upon God's love for us, Jesus said, "My yoke is easy, my burden is light." Christians experience God as one who loves all of humanity so much as to die for us. The love of the cross has always been the way God loves us. St. John says that Jesus is our advocate. Our prayers do not make God care for us or take notice of us. Jesus is the proof that God does not need to be asked for help.

Then why pray? Because praying is trusting. Consider love between two people. In order for that love to grow it needs to be

5

expressed. Simply to hold the thought intellectually without the manifestation of the thought in tangible ways by word and deed risks destroying the mutual love at worst and, at best, making the love irrelevant to daily life. One may say, "I don't need to say 'I love you' because you know it." To which the other might respond, "How do I know if I see no evidence of it?" Praying is our way of expressing tangibly the love of God and nurturing the love within ourselves and our relationships. It is one of the most important ways of putting our faith to work.

How can you be sure that God answers prayers? The real question is whether you can be sure that God loves those for whom you pray. If you are secure in the love of God then you will neither worry nor feel burned-out. The more you pray and exercise your faith, you will be assured of God's faithfulness in return.

I suspect that you feel more secure in the love of God than you do in your ability to pray. I suggest that you simply trust more in that love and pray with self-abandoned joy in God's love for those in your prayers. Prayer is not intended to protect us from sharing the burdens and sorrows of others, but it is God's gift to help us endure our trials with wisdom, compassion and undying hope.

You can be sure that God answers prayer because God is love.

How do I know that God answers prayer?

In Matthew 7:9-11, Jesus says, "If your child asks for bread, would you give him a stone? If he asks for a fish, would you give him a serpent? As bad as you are, you know how to give good things to your children. How much more, then, will your Father in heaven give good things to those who ask him!" We know that God answers prayer because God is the source of the love we share as human beings.

This does not mean, of course, that we always get that for which we ask. Let me describe a hypothetical situation. You ask God to help you find a lost pair of glasses, and suddenly you find them in a spot you had looked before but didn't see them. You would probably say this is answered prayer because you found your glasses.

We sometimes literally get what we ask for and we sometimes

don't. When we do, our faith is strengthened. When we don't, we are tempted to doubt ourselves or God. In effect, we are depending upon the sign, the object of our prayer, as the basis for our faith.

Jesus warned us about that when he said strongly, "An evil and adulterous generation asks for a sign." He also said, "Blessed are those who have not seen and yet have come to believe."

If we are depending upon the sign for the evidence of answered prayer, then we know when the prayer is answered by the sign. Many do not believe because they think of answered prayer in such a way and refuse to overlook the reality that many, if not most prayers, do not result in such divine intervention.

Many do not accept Jesus as the Messiah for a similar reason. If he were, it is alleged, then the Hebrew prophecies of peace and the end of suffering would have been fulfilled. Since this obviously has not happened in the world, even briefly, Jesus cannot be the expected one.

As long as we are waiting for such literal responses as the only answers to prayer and fulfillment of hope, we are not trusting in God. In Hebrews 11:1 we are told, "Faith is the substance of things hoped for, the evidence of things unseen." Faith offers so much more than signs. Faith enlivens the Holy Spirit, the very presence of God.

Returning to the hypothetical situation, we experience many answers whether the glasses are found or not. First, we are reminded that we are not alone. To pray is to join in the choir of angels and the communion of saints. It is opening the window and letting the light in. It is breathing the freshness of a clear, damp morning after a rainstorm, or that first gasp of air after being under water to one's limit. Prayer gives life to our souls just as oxygen gives life to our bodies. Concern over the lost glasses pales in the comfort of God's peaceful embrace.

Second, the assurance of God's presence helps us to respond to any situation with a calmer and wiser perspective. In the case of the glasses, it may simply be that the second look in a previous location was more relaxed and confident that the glasses were where they should have been. And so they are. My daughter once described that she felt so relaxed taking an exam after a short prayer that she was able to think more clearly and recall what she had studied.

Prayer can also remind us of God's call to be loving, and help us to respond as Jesus might, rather than from our perspective of fear or anger.

Prayer will also help us maintain hope. Hope to a person who prays is not wishful thinking. Rather, it is confidence in the future because it belongs to God. Christian hope is based on the understanding that Jesus Christ, who loved without counting the cost and forgave from the cross, reveals the nature of God, the source and ruler of all.

God always answers prayer because with every prayer a sense of God's presence is enlivened, faith is given power, and we are reminded of our destiny. Sometimes we do receive signs and literal answers, but these are not the precious things.

My husband has been ill for a long time and suffered greatly. Is it O.K. to pray for his death?

Your question indicates a deep struggle with some of the thoughts people of faith have when in the midst of trial.

On one hand, we want to trust and not ask God to remove trials from us. We know that hardships can be the testing ground of faith, and as painful as the situation may be, we want to be proven worthy and grow in our relationship with God. Where would we be if Jesus had not been willing to endure the trial of his passion and death so that God could save the world through him? Bravely, we resist the easy way out.

On the other hand, God knows our hearts, and if it is our wish for ourselves or a loved one to be removed from suffering, should it not be our prayer? It is important not to censor our prayers to be what we think is appropriate for God's ears or will make us look good in the eyes of God. Honesty is an essential step toward intimacy with God, and by being honest we often sense movement toward healing, strength, and acceptance without resignation.

In the midst of such a dilemma, try to maintain your perspective. This can be done by remembering that there are different kinds of prayer. In your present situation, it would be easy to let your only prayer be a prayer of intercession. You want to ask God to take your husband and remove his suffering. You are understandably overwhelmed by the illness of your husband and it is hard to see anything else. But if you remember that there are other forms of prayer, your prayer of intercession will be in a larger and critically important context.

Other forms of prayer include Adoration, Confession, Thanksgiving, and Supplication. (You can remember the forms easily by using the word, "ACTS.") Supplication includes both petition and intercession. Praying for your husband would be a prayer of intercession. Praying for yourself would be a prayer of petition.

One of the reasons for setting time aside for prayer is that you can pray more intentionally all of the forms of prayer. In praying for your husband, for example, you can begin with adoration. Another word for adoration is praise. It is different from a thanksgiving prayer in that we are not specific in our prayer. We simply praise God as creatures made in the image of God. To praise is to acknowledge the holiness of God, to express our trust, and to honor the place of God in our lives. It is not unusual to sing prayers of praise, or to simply meditate upon the sacred presence of God who has promised to be with you. Praising lifts our souls into the reality of God's presence.

After a time of praise, many enter a time of confession. In your need, it would be appropriate for you to bare your desire that your husband's pain come to an end. It is helpful to be in touch with your anger with the fact of your husband's illness and God's apparent unwillingness to heal him. Confession is good for the soul not because it informs God, but because it helps us face ourselves. Admitting what we think God would not like in us opens God's forgiveness because it is the beginning of forgiving ourselves.

You might thank God for the gift of life and of love, particularly the love you share as wife and husband. You know that illness and even death cannot separate you from the love of God, and you can thank God in Christ for entering into the suffering of our humanity and for the resurrection of Jesus which promises a new life for your husband as well.

Don't forget the prayer of petition. This is to pray for yourself. Perhaps it would be for the wisdom and courage to say what would be most loving and helpful to your husband and family. It may be for understanding. Certainly it would be for strength.

Finally, you are ready to pray for your husband in the context appropriate to your faith. If you have taken the time to imbed your intercessory prayer in the full gift of prayer, you may not have answers, but you will certainly have what is more important - faith, hope, and love.

My husband has been painfully ill for thirteen years and is now suffering horribly. I want the Lord to take him. Is it a sin to pray for release?

No, it is not a sin to pray for your husband to die under these circumstances. You should not add to your burden by feeling guilt for wanting your husband to be relieved of the pain and take that next step which death offers toward his Lord and God. God honors your love for your husband and your desire for him to receive what has been described as the "ultimate healing."

When we say "I want the Lord to take him," it is important to understand that our Lord does not cause people to die. While death must be included as a part of life, it is not that God initiates the causes of death. Think, for example, from a child's perspective when she hears upon her mother's sudden death that "God took her to heaven." In the effort to comfort her, we are actually creating an understandable hostility toward God and mistrust of life. It is much better to be frank and factual about why people die. Mommy got sick, or there was an accident. Children can handle these realities better than we think, and our ability to talk openly about them without the sugar coating of blaming God will help them develop a stronger faith.

Likewise, in your situation, it would be a mistake to blame God for your husband's prolonged illness. In addition to the agony of suffering through such times, people will wrongly add the torture of wondering why God has selected them for unusual suffering. They may feel that it is God's punishment, and feel not only the pain but also the responsibility. Or, they may feel that God is testing them. Some may even take pride in their lot because they rationalize that God has selected them for martyrdom.

All of these are ways of attempting to deal with suffering in our lives. We cope as best we can. But we can see the image of God they project. Words like frightening, dangerously mysterious, capricious, punishing, testing, and harsh come to mind. But if we realize that God does not overtly bring such suffering into the world, then it is not a matter of trying to figure out why, but of seeking God's grace to respond appropriately.

There are many reasons for suffering and death, natural, or created by the sinful choices humans make, or simply accidental. When someone dies and we say that God "took them" we really mean that God's love for us does not allow death to take us away. Jesus proclaims such love when he says in John 14:2,3 "In my Father's house are many rooms; if it were not so, would I have told you that I go to prepare a place for you? And when I go and prepare a place for you, I will come again and will take you to myself, that where I am you may be also."

When there is suffering and death, it is not God who causes it, but it is God who is there to take us by the hand and walk through with us to the fulfillment of Jesus' promise. Because of the resurrection of Jesus, we can respond with a resounding yes to his invitation which begins the 14th Chapter of John, "Let not your hearts be troubled."

We can understand that you want your husband to realize the fullness of that promise as soon as possible. Know that he will. Jesus will be there to meet him when he dies and to raise him up to that new life which is to come.

> *I've been praying with no effect for my daughter's healing, and I'm feeling hopeless. Why doesn't God answer my prayer?*

The recent death of a premature baby born to a family I know caused me to reflect on the meaning of Christian hope. Your prayers may be based on your own hopes rather than hope in God.

"....a little child shall lead them." This prophecy from the Book of Isaiah is cherished by Christians as the foretelling of the Christ child, and is one of the readings in the common lectionary for Advent. As I met and prayed with the family of little Henry, I realized that God was using Henry in a powerful way to lead them closer to God although his life was only a matter of hours.

Christian hope is not about feelings, but knowledge. We would be less than honest if we did not feel hopeless at times. The reality of illness and death can overwhelm us when they hit close to home, and we would be less than honest if we did not pray to God to remove them from us. Yet, as we pray, we also know through Christ that God is with us in our joys and our sorrows. Whether our lives are only a few hours, as Henry's was, or a hundred years, God is with us and God's time is eternal. Even a century is but a blink of God's eye. Our hope therefore is not placed in the survival of that which is temporary, but in the love of that which is eternal.

Second, hope is not about our desires, but about faith. When my children were small, their prayer always included the word, "hope." They would say, "I hope that Grandma will get well." All prayers, if honest, express our desires. But even as we pray we know that God has already answered our prayer far beyond ways we can imagine. So we pray with trust that God is good, cares for us and all people, and that in the end, as Julian of Norwich said in the midst of her own suffering, "All is well. All is exceedingly well."

Third, hope is not about the future alone, but also the present. This came home powerfully to me as I struggled for meaning in the midst of Henry's struggle for life. He had no future in this world, yet he was a member of the Body of Christ. Jesus said, "What you do to these the least of my brethren, you do to me." As his parents held Henry lovingly in their arms, they were holding Christ. And God ministered to this family through Henry. They were deeply touched by God, their faith was strengthened, and ironically, their capacity for gratitude was greatly expanded. In the midst of grief, they were drawn closer to one another and to God in gratitude. The greatest saint could not have given this family anything more important than what little Henry gave them in only a few hours. Christian hope has a future dimension, certainly, as God leads us toward the fullness of the Kingdom, but it is also a very present reality as God works through us now to bring heaven to earth.

Finally, hope is not about waiting for God to act for us, but working with God to act through us. If God could do so much through

Henry, how much more can God accomplish in the here and now through our lives, with all of our experience, wisdom, and resources? We sometimes feel we have so little to offer, or that we cannot risk what we have because we may not have enough. These fearful thoughts prevent us from allowing God to use us to bring love into our communities and the world.

Our prayers sometimes seem to go unanswered, but Christian hope tells us that God has come to dwell with us in the midst of our sorrow. We might look at our lives or the lives of those for whom we pray and feel hopeless at what they have come to. But the Incarnation which we celebrate at Christmas says not to look at what our lives have come to, but at what has come into our lives.

When I try to pray, I feel so inept. Can you help?

You already have the most important ingredient in prayer: the desire. Everything else pales by comparison. Purity of heart, the humble soul longing for God, is all that one needs for prayer to be Spirit-filled and powerful. While techniques and discipline can enhance your prayers, these can also be empty forms without the sincere desire to spend time with the Lord.

However, since you are not experiencing fulfillment in your prayers, let me suggest some of the reasons people feel dry in their prayer life. It is really a matter of understanding.

To feel inept is appropriate. Your question comes from a male perspective, and it is not easy for many men to express feelings. It is not easy to even know what our emotions are. So your feelings of ineptness tell me that you have reached a level in your desire to pray where you are not simply petitioning God, but are probing for intimacy with God. This is holy ground, not easy even with another human being.

To feel inept is ongoing. While most of us feel increasingly at ease in the presence of God through prayer, we are also ever drawn into the divine mystery in ways that we seldom understand, anticipate or accept initially. To pray sincerely is to invite God to transform us, to make us new. Newness is uncomfortable even when we know where God is leading. Usually, we know that we don't know, and that is very uncomfortable, indeed.

To feel inept is to trust. It would feel safer to have tools at hand which guarantee the results of our prayer. If it were that easy, we would be in the position of manipulating God. But to pray is to place ourselves at God's disposal. We would not want to do that unless we trusted God with our lives. Jesus asks us to trust him, and his words and actions reveal a God who loves humanity so much as to die for us.

When we feel inept in prayer, we can remind ourselves that the quality and the results of our prayer do not depend upon us, but upon a God who loves us more than we can imagine. It is in this framework that Jesus says to us, "Ask and it shall be given to you." To ask from the perspective of one who knows the love of Jesus is to know that whatever good we seek is surpassed by the good which God offers. We may feel inept in the asking, but we trust the answer of a creator who is also our friend.

To feel inept is to grow. There is a danger in developing techniques which work for us. When we become too comfortable or successful in a nurturing prayer life, it is time to ask ourselves if we have been growing lately. Have we become too attached to the form and lost the substance? Is the meaning in prayer derived from the rhythm, the balance, the beauty, the sense of gratification that we have fulfilled an obligation? Or, does meaning flow from knowing that we have encountered God?

A word of caution here: One will not have that overwhelming sense of God's presence always in prayer. It will probably not exist in the majority of prayer moments. We accept God's presence on faith even when we don't feel it. Nevertheless, it is important to examine our prayer life regularly to be sure that we have not become attached to our prayers rather than to God.

Jesus said that the Kingdom of God is upon us. He also said that we must receive it like a child in order to enter it. Your inadequate feelings may be the child in you reaching for God while the adult wishes to be in control. Take Jesus' advice. Go with your child.

14

Why do people pray for the dead? Do they really need our prayers? And if they do, isn't it too late for them?

We pray for the dead because God is the God of the living and the dead. The Bible teaches us that death does not separate us from the love of God. Just as we pray for one another in this life, it is appropriate to pray for those who have died.

Your question can be addressed by discussing what life is. The most common understanding of life is a biological one. The body is alive when it functions biologically, and when the biological process stops, it is dead. We pray for healing of the body when someone is alive, but there would be no point in continuing to pray for someone after death if the only interpretation of life were its physical meaning.

There is another sense of what life is, however. It is life of a different order than the physical, which we call spiritual. The spiritual order of being is not dependent upon the physical for its existence. While the body is the vessel through which we become aware of God's gift of life, both physical and spiritual, we see through the limitations of the body to a life beyond which transforms us and gives us hope beyond the grave.

The prime concern for people of faith is, of course, spiritual life. This is why Jesus said things like, "If your eye causes you to stumble, tear it out and throw it away; it is better for you to enter life (physical) with one eye than to have two eyes and be thrown into the hell of fire (spiritual)."

Jesus uses hyperbole here to make the point that the spiritual life, our relationship with God, contains infinitely more blessing than whatever temporal pleasures we might find in the physical realm.

We pray, then, for those who have died because we want them to continue to grow in the spiritual life. We begin to experience eternal life in the world through our relationship with God. We also pray for the dead because it reminds us that in God's love, death does not separate us ultimately from them.

Both the living and the dead make up what the church calls the "communion of saints." To pray for them strengthens us by reminding us of our inheritance of fellowship in this "great cloud of witnesses," as St. Paul describes those who have gone before us. It assures us of our creator's love beyond the grave, and of the duty we have to make the most of our lives while we continue in this world.

As we pray for the dead, it is important to understand that we are not praying for their salvation. That prayer has already been made for all people and for all times by Jesus: "Father, forgive them for they know not what they do." We can trust in Jesus' prayer for ourselves and those for whom we pray because he has expressed the very heart of God.

We pray simply because we care. We want to commend our loved ones continually to God's loving providence. Praying for the dead also places our own lives in the larger context of a love that passes human understanding, yet is very real. It brings before our eyes the heritage loved ones have given us, and imbues that heritage with eternal significance.

It might be said that when we pray for the dead, we are not praying for the dead at all, but for those who are more fully alive. By continuing to be aware of our connection with them through God's love, we keep our eyes upon the goal and are helped to fight the fight of faith.

Praying for the dead does as much for us as for them. By keeping us focused on eternal realities, such prayer helps us to invest ourselves in the spiritual treasure of God's love. Have no fear of praying for the dead. What we really need to fear is the temptation of the idea that biological life is all there is.

SPIRITUAL GROWTH

*Could you answer the fol-
lowing question: "Why do you believe in God?"*

This may surprise you, but I believe because I choose to. And I suspect most people do. If people are waiting until they have proof for the existence of God, then they will never cross the threshold of faith. As the Book of Hebrews tells us, "Faith is the assurance of things hoped for, the conviction of things not seen."

While philosophers and theologians have attempted to provide ontological proof for the existence of God, they agree that ultimately one must respond to revelation rather than empirical evidence alone.

St. Thomas Aquinas, at the beginning of the Fifth Century, postulated five arguments for the existence of God, one of them being if the universe gives evidence of order and design, there must be a designer. Another is the "first mover" argument. Everything in creation moves because something else has moved it. Even if we stretch this back to the "big bang", what caused that to happen? Well, you get the idea.

I wonder what you mean by your question. If you mean do I believe that God exists, I would have to say yes, given all of the evidence. But I realize that the evidence is not conclusive, and never can be. Therefore, intellectual integrity demands that I allow for the possibility that God does not exist. But if you are asking why I place my trust in God (which is the true meaning of belief) I respond that by trusting I have met what is beyond myself and our humanity.

19

As a Christian, I have experienced the grace and power of God through Jesus Christ. I find in that relationship more than the study of an historical figure. It is living with God whom I know through the historical person of Jesus and the inspired witness of him in Scripture and the Christian community.

In the Fourth Century, St. Augustine captured the essence of believing when he said, "I seek not to understand so that I can believe, but to believe so that I can understand." He chose, therefore, to believe. The understanding followed. This is the way of faith. It requires in its initial step that "leap of faith," a phrase credited to Soren Kierkegaard.

For me, the leap of faith is not an irrational one. In fact, its healthy growth requires intellectual integrity. First, I find the ontological proofs convincing, although there is reasonable room for doubt. Second, and more importantly, once one "lets go" of the need for certainty the proof comes in the experience which follows.

Giving one's self to God is, of course, very personal. Yet, one is assured through both anthropology and sociology that the spiritual experience is as much a part of our humanity as any scientific certainty.

For those who doubt, I ask them to ponder the experience of love. While it cannot be empirically proven, no one would question the fact of its existence and its power. Further, no one experiences love without letting go of the demand for proof.

> *I've always been interested in the fact that religious people don't seem to be much different than non-religious people. In fact, a case could be made that when people "get religion" they become less tolerant and loving that the rest of the community. Why doesn't faith have a more obvious positive influence upon people?*

I'm tempted to argue with your premise, but since what you suggest is certainly true in some cases, I'll address it at face value. People can become worse rather than better because of religious conversion.

Religious conversion is not enough. We may awaken to the

powerful experience of salvation, but that does not mean that we are wholly God's. Rather, the important question should be, "What does this new awareness mean for my life?"

Don Gelpi, a Jesuit professor at the Graduate Theological Union in Berkeley while I was there, first introduced me to the concept of conversion as a process which must integrate the emotions, the intellect, and the behavior of a person.

Emotional Conversion: Most people experience faith through their feelings. For some it is a gradual emotional attachment with a church or synagogue because they grew up with it. They simply wouldn't be who they are without the faith given to them by their families and significant people in their lives. Others have dramatic emotional conversions at a certain place and time. They know the moment they "were saved."

Emotional conversion is falling in love with God. Crucial and powerful as it may be, it is also dangerously seductive because we tend to associate the power of the experience with the circumstances in which we received it. For instance, if conversion happened on a retreat, then we may feel that we have to go on retreat in order to experience it again. Or, we may get locked into a certain denomination or religion as the key to the experience. We always need to take a reality check on where we place our emotional attachment. Is it truly upon God, or is it upon the package through which we have experienced God?

Intellectual Conversion: Many people feel that the rational mind is a threat to their faith. They will study their faith, but only within certain parameters. To them, some things are sacred and beyond question. For example, many will not entertain the idea that Moses may not have actually written the first five books of the Bible which are traditionally attributed to him. While aware of modern scholarship, they choose not to give it value. To do so would be to undermine their absolute acceptance of what the Bible says.

Intellectual conversion really means that all aspects of one's faith are open to inquiry and challenge. This does not imply that the rational mind rules supreme, but that it cannot be suspended at any stage of the conversion process.

Moral Conversion: We all know people who believe in God but do not practice fully what they believe. We only have to look in the mirror! It is one thing to accept God as our savior, and quite another to accept God as our Lord. Yet we know that faith is not so much what we hold in our heads as what we say with our tongues and do with our hands. To the extent that we do not do what our faith commands we are not morally converted.

If that doesn't humble us enough, it must be said that moral conversion is not simply a matter of doing what God says to do. External behavior is, of course, important, but it is not enough. Again, the motive is the key to religious morality. In what kind of spirit and for what reason do we do what we do? If our motive is primarily self-serving, we will most likely be morally wrong even while complying with the letter of the law. Likewise, we may violate the letter of the law in order to perform an act of love and be morally right.

Your point that people should be affected in positive ways because they are religious is well taken. The fact that many aren't is because they are not taking responsibility for one or more of these three aspects of the conversion process.

How do I know God's will?
I have to decide whether to accept a good position with
a company which would involve lots of travel and less
time with my family. I'm torn, and would like to know
what God wants me to do.

It's always difficult to make important decisions when the alternatives have both an up and a down side. Close communication with those we love, thorough examination of the facts and not rushing the decision are all important. God uses such practical steps to reveal the best choices to us.

Your question implies that there is one choice which is God's will and only one. This places you under pressure in an already difficult decision to be sure you do God's will. In any decision each option has its cost. There is no perfect choice, usually, and hopefully our choices are a matter of doing what is most right and least wrong.

You need, therefore, to be easier on yourself, pray for guidance, and use your best judgment after as much research and consultation with loved ones as you can. Then go for it. Know that God is with you in your decision, and that the process you have used may reveal to you ways to minimize any negative effects of your decision.

Our choices are important to God because they affect the quality of our lives and the world we live in. Some things are clear. The Ten Commandments, for example, state clearly the kinds of things which God does not want us to do. Jesus' teaching is full of examples of what God does want us to do. His life and the teaching of the early church recorded in the Bible give us a lot of guidance on what the love of God looks like. Yet there are still times, such as the one you are now facing, when the answer is not obvious.

Following the Spirit of God in the daily choices of our lives is a learned discipline. Let me describe for you some of its elements.

Establish an active relationship with God. The building blocks of such a relationship are prayer, study, and action. It is a matter of growing stronger each day in our spiritual lives because we take the time to listen to God in our private devotions and corporate worship. We learn about God by reading and learning from the lessons in life, and we serve God through our actions. This ongoing habit of being in the presence of God, sometimes called the Rule of Life, is the essence of acquiring the kind of maturity which will be available to us when we face forks in the road.

Find a spiritual director of friend. There is great value in having someone with whom we can articulate our emerging sensitivity to the Holy Spirit. Find one who will not be the kind of person who gives advice or tries to control you, but someone whose maturity and wisdom allows him or her to listen, to ask appropriate questions which help you explore possibilities, to support you unfailingly, and to encourage you with faith in your capacity for spiritual growth. Such a person may be hard to find, but most people never look.

You may want to form a spiritual friendship with someone you trust and learn together how to be spiritual mentors for one another. A helpful book with good resources is "Mentoring: The Ministry of Spiritual Kinship," by Edward C. Sellner, published by Ave Maria Press. A word of caution: The relationship I describe needs to have clear boundaries. Complete honesty, openness, and trust can lead to romantic feelings if the seeds of that are present. Be clear with yourself about your intentions and stay within your purpose.

Find a community of faith. Each of us finds our true calling in the context of community. St. Paul used the analogy of the human body. Think of yourself, for example, as an arm. Detached from the rest of the body, an arm would have all of its gifts, but how would it know what to do with them? And without the rest of the body, the arm could not perform its function at all. We need the gifts of others. We need the challenge of relationships with others different from ourselves, while working toward a common purpose.

We don't have to reinvent the wheel. The wisdom of our tradition doesn't restrict us. It releases us to add our unique contribution to the beautiful building already begun and proven to have withstood the storms of centuries. If you're not already in a worshipping community, find one that you feel will nurture you and help you to discern the Spirit of God in your life.

Churches and synagogues consist of sincere, ordinary people seeking to grow in their faith and make a difference in the world around them. We don't need to be told what to do by our church; we need to learn how to hear the voice of God ourselves.

> *At my Bible study a friend took out some "angel cards" and we all drew a card which became our "message for the day." Is this sort of thing appropriate for Christians?*

Your question raises the issue of how people of faith seek guidance and knowledge from God. While it would be nice to think that all we have to do is to draw a card, or randomly open a page of the Bible, or go to a psychic to hear God's word to us, the Spirit usually works from within our own relationship with God. Things or people outside of yourself may be used as stimulus for meditation, but it is unwise to give them inherent power.

First of all, any card in the deck would probably have the effect of seeming to be exactly what that person needs. That's the nature of the good thoughts contained there. Second, true guidance from God is the fruit of a prayerful process of integrating your knowledge of scripture, the teaching of your faith tradition, and your own life's experiences.

The path of the spiritual journey is inward. It is gradually releasing one's self to the presence of the Holy Spirit, and learning to draw from those living waters. Clinging to outside authority in matters of faith causes one to remain immature spiritually, dependent upon that authority, and vulnerable to potential abuse.

Each of us is a child of God and capable, with sincere devotion and continuing practice, of discerning God's will.

Your faith community is an important place to find the tools and nourishment to sustain your interior journey, but even your community cannot be the final word in terms of your own relationship with God.

Personal conscience always prevails, even over the authority of your faith community. This is why it is so important for each of us to responsibly and lovingly develop the level of maturity in our faith which will empower our decisions and make us full contributing members to the spiritual consciousness of our community.

Never surrender the difficult and sometimes ambiguous task of soul-searching for the quick-fix of a definitive answer, least of all the answer provided through a random pick.

Having said that, it must also be said that almost anything can be used as a stimulus for the inward journey. One might ponder the wonders of nature or the complexities of a relationship, or reflect upon words or pictures, however chosen. Julian of Norwich received spiritual nourishment by meditating upon an acorn, and poet Robert Blake saw eternity in a grain of sand. But there's a big difference between using something as a stimulus to know God within and giving power to something outside of yourself which is not God.

Angel cards are fun as a parlor game, but hardly the stuff of which a strong spiritual life is made.

Sometimes I experience times of spiritual emptiness. How do I get back in touch with God during these times?

Even though we know we are not the first person to experience such times, when we are in the midst of them, they can be very despairing. Remember that even nature provides many examples of life where there seems to be no life. The dry Saltan Sea or the mountain's dry rainwater pool await only the stimulus of water from the heavens to become surging miniature ecosystems. The dry period is not an impediment to the survival of these mysterious creatures; it is essential.

This is also true for us, although dry periods are not usually pleasant. They are part of the gift of life, and need to be taken in stride. For writers, it is writer's block. For lovers, it can be the absence of passion. For people of faith, it is the sense that God is remote and inaccessible. Like the cocoon which conceals the butterfly, these times contain the beauty of life in its formative stages.

Tremendous spiritual growth is actually occurring when we feel the absence of God. When Jesus said, "Blessed are the poor in spirit, for their is the kingdom of heaven," I think he was giving us a word of strength for such times, and inviting us to trust God when it seems we have no logical reason to do so.

It is when we are truly on our knees that our longing for God becomes more than academic. We realize then that we desperately need a relationship with God. Ironically, the experience of God is most near when we feel alone.

The prophet Elijah experienced such a time. The wilderness experience was apparently necessary for Elijah to hear God. Likewise, Jesus' ministry began with such a wilderness experience of forty days and forty nights.

Here are some suggestions for when you're feeling desperate and alone.

- Remember that despair is a normal part of what it is to be human. Hidden in the experience is heavenly treasure.

- Allow yourself the freedom of trusting God completely. Say out loud or write on paper your feelings in a conversation with God.

It's not only okay to trust God when we have no where else to turn, but that's what God hopes we will do.

- Find someone to talk to. God uses friends and counselors to give us strength and perspective. This may be a good time to get to know your pastor better.

- Help someone. Restore a sense of vitality by making a positive difference in the life of someone else, even a stranger.

- Finally, be patient with yourself. Know that while you may not see results right away, you are growing in faith, and that is the greatest reward of all.

I got into a friendly argument the other day with a friend who says that the only thing that matters to God is that we do good in our lives. I think doing good is fine, but that we also must accept Jesus Christ as our Lord and Savior to be saved. What do you think?

I'm glad to hear your argument was friendly! Often we lose a spirit of friendship discussing religious issues. We need to practice the ability to share deeply felt matters of faith without feeling threatened. Ultimate truths can be addressed in a climate of friendship if we realize that our perceptions are limited and serious discussion helps us to have a greater understanding.

Your question raises the controversy of faith versus works. The thrust of Christian faith is that works alone do not save us. Rather, we are saved because God loves us unconditionally. Trusting in that fact is what faith is. On the other hand, such faith is worthless if it is not expressed in loving actions toward others. As St. John says, "If you say you love God and hate your neighbor, you are a liar." Faith and service are two sides of the same coin.

The underlying question is this, "What does it mean to be saved?" One answer might be that to be saved means one is "going to heaven." This focuses upon our future relationship with God, and sets God up as a judge who will decide between those accepted into heaven and those who are not. Our decisions, expressed through faith or service, or both, are in this scenario the evidence used by God to let us in or keep us out.

Another way to think of salvation is in the past tense. Let's assume for the sake of conversation that we are already destined for heaven as a gift to us from God. It doesn't matter, in this case, what we believe or what we do. Everyone is included, presumably because God wants it that way, and will not let our shortcomings, whatever they are, stand in the way. This universal acceptance implies the opposite of the first scenario. Here, God does not care what we do or believe, at least not enough to build into the overall plan any consequences.

In the first instance, God has great expectations and will judge us; in the second, God has no expectations, and makes no judgments. The first is very controlling, the second is apathetic.

But there is a third possibility. Think of God as one who loves. This is the God at the core of all religions and the God experienced dramatically in the life of Jesus. Here, salvation is seen neither as a reward for good behavior nor a given fact of human life, but rather a dynamic relationship between ourselves and God. With every human being the invitation is extended to enter into a loving relationship with God and with others whom God also loves. Salvation is knowing God as one's creator and faithful friend. It is a quality of life derived from a sure identity, a purpose for living, and trust in the future, even beyond the grave.

What then, does this understanding of salvation as a loving relationship with God have to say about your question? If salvation means that we know God loves us and seeks to have a meaningful relationship with us, then certainly we must say that good works alone are not all that God wants of us. God also wants our hearts. On the other hand, if we say that God has our heart but we do little to live in God's love, then we must question, as St. John does, whether we speak the truth.

Good works are not important because they earn us any status with God. Our status with God is given. God loves us and that is that. Good works are important because they are one of the two ways through which we return our love to God. The other, of course, is worship.

*Could you please lend your perspec-
tive on the various apparitions of the Virgin Mary? Why
does she only appear to Roman Catholics? How valid
do you think these Marian experiences are?*

Mary, the mother of Jesus, is highly revered in catholic tradition because she is the "God bearer" for the world. She is the
supreme example of a human being's joyful submission to the Holy
Spirit. She represents the ideal in Christian ministry by her trust
in God and her willingness to allow herself to be a means of God's
grace entering into human history.

Over the centuries tradition has deduced doctrine from the
biblical information about Mary which attributes to her qualities
similar to Christ himself. For example, the Doctrine of the Im-
maculate Conception states that she was, from her conception, without sin. Also, the Doctrine of the Assumption states that she did
not die, but was "assumed" into heaven. The Protestant movement
of the Reformation sought largely to return to the literal scriptural
accounts and has tended to view Mary without the doctrines of
Roman or Eastern (Orthodox) traditions.

The point is that Mary is special, whether viewed in the fullness of her humanity as Protestants do, or with divine attributes
as Romans and Orthodox Christians have traditionally done. Where
intense devotion to Mary has been emphasized there have been
many of the apparitions you mention.

Familiar examples have been at Lourdes, Fatima, and in recent years at Medugorje in Yugoslavia. The Virgin of Guadalupe is
revered by the Mexican-American community and the Madonna del
Sasso by the Swiss.

It would be unwise to discount apparitions of Mary because
of the lack scientific evidence or because of what we have learned
about psychology. To put it simply, people of faith experience an
intangible dimension of life neither evident to others nor submissive to the laws of science.

Dramatic experiences of faith are very real, yet unexplain-
able in modern scientific terms. Furthermore, history shows that
religious experiences, including apparitions, can bring dramatic

healing and transformation into people's lives. This is not to say that claims of such apparitions are always authentic. We know all too well the ability of our minds to see what we want to see, and of the will of some to exploit the faith of others.

Apart from the question of the validity of the apparitions of Mary, I am reminded of Jesus' impatient reaction to those who asked for signs in order to believe. Faith which requires proof is not faith at all. Our "guarantee" is the presence of the Holy Spirit within those who trust God and are called according to God's purpose.

While a source of inspiration, excessive devotion to the saints can distract us from nurturing our personal relationship with God. The saints are before us as examples, but they are not the ones who heal or save us, not even Mary, as great as she is in the human response to God.

Have you run across people
who want so badly to believe, but can't - and so become
hostile? I suspect it's rather common.

I suspect there are many people who are hostile to faith because they simply don't sense those urgings within themselves which they perceive others to have. Hostility is also engendered by the abuses of churches and clergy that are all too evident in our world today.

If you were such a person, I would respond to you this way: First, I would explore what you mean by the word, "believe." Second, I would ask you to share the experiences you have had which brought you to your present understanding of faith. Finally, I would try to help you honor yourself and your feelings, whatever they may be, and trust that upon this foundation you can build your faith. The key is your desire to believe.

What do you mean by faith? We all have faith in something. A good word to substitute for faith is trust. Where do you place your trust? Many trust no one but themselves. Others may place their ultimate trust in a relationship, or in financial security, or in a healthy lifestyle or any combination of the above. In our sickest moments, we misplace our trust in the abuse of alcohol or drugs.

The decision to have faith is not a matter of choosing this or that religion. It is a matter of asking yourself where you place your ultimate trust. What is your highest power? What gives ultimate meaning to your life?

Having asked yourself that question in brutal honesty, you can decide if it is really appropriate to place your trust there. Is the object of your trust truly trustworthy? Or, is it as subject to the transitory character of life as you are?

Faith is simply the desire to engage with the eternal. In a word, God. It is not agreement to a doctrine, membership in an organization or surrender of your being to worldly authorities. We might submit ourselves to such worldly resources because they are part of the tools of faith, but surrender is reserved for God alone.

What experiences have you had which brought you to your present understanding of faith?

We are all the products of our environment to a large degree. A person seeking faith or a deepening of faith is wise to reflect upon one's personal history of faith or lack of it.

If a person feels blocked in a relationship with God, there is most certainly a reason. The myth is that because faith is a gift, some have it, some don't. The reality is that we are all made in the image of God. A relationship with God is part of the gift of being human. If we're not experiencing it, then there is a reason.

I know a person who was told as a child that God was for sissies and old ladies. I know another who experienced at a tender age a drunken grandfather on Christmas Eve telling frightening stories about God ending the world. Many people can tell stories of such religious abuse.

Other blockages may be more conscious struggles with the realities of the world. "If God exists, why is there so much evil and suffering?" Still others may simply have received a lack of stimulation and encouragement in a relationship with God and, like the child who never learned to swim, avoid the deep water.

Honor yourself and your feelings. I have found that many people think of faith as having to be like someone else or a group of people who they assume think a certain way. They receive the impression that there is one way of believing because most believers present their faith as "The True Faith." Sensitive to the arrogance in this, they reject the path of faith altogether.

31

Also, they may know people who seem to be in "loving communion" with God, and because they don't feel that, they feel empty. In reality, even the most devout struggle with these issues. None of us, if we are honest, is always close to God. Some may never feel close to God, but still trust God and keep the connection alive. These may be the most faithful of all.

I leave you with a poignant quote from a teacher in the Anglican Christian tradition, Evelyn Underhill: "Mystics are not loved and attended to by God more than us, but they love and attend to God more than we do."

My father was a wonderful, loving man, but never accepted Christ to my knowledge because of the harsh way he was treated by his church as a child. Do you think he will be resurrected from the dead and go to heaven?

The answer to your question is unequivocally yes. My response is based upon the love of Jesus Christ, who is the way, the truth, and the life. His resurrection from the dead is God's promise to humanity of love which has victory over the grave. If there were any other criteria for getting into heaven than the unconditional love of Jesus, I would not be able to answer the question so surely.

People often hold concern for the salvation of loved ones. The best thing to do if you are concerned is to trust. Know that God loves that person even more than you do, and that nothing can separate him or her from the love of God. You may have expended all of your best efforts to bring about the person's conversion and failed. But God will keep trying.

As you imply, we cannot know what is truly in the heart of another person. Many people reject the outward forms of religion because their experience of it has been negative, even abusive, but this does not mean they reject God. Without the form of the church, they simply know no way of manifesting their devotion except through their loving deeds. They are known to God by the fruit they bear in their lives.

So have no concern for your father's salvation. You may grieve for what he did not enjoy in his life, the knowledge of Jesus Christ as his Lord and Savior. But do not grieve for him now. Like all of us will when the time comes, he now sees clearly.

Does this mean that everyone will automatically go to heaven? Of course, no one knows, but it seems to me that God will not exclude people who have never really had a fair opportunity to say yes to God. People like your father quite legitimately rejected his experience of the church because it was not true to the love of Christ. But, of course, he didn't know that. Others may never have the opportunity to hear about God's love.

Will this be held against them? Many belong to cultures which are simply not Christian, and although they may know of Christianity, they are steeped in their own religious tradition. They are devoted to God, but not Christian. It is arrogant for Christians to think that non-Christians are loved any less. More than that, it is unfaithful. We believe that Jesus is the only way, but we violate the way by excluding those outside our particular traditions.

The whole matter of salvation is not about the future, but the present. It is better for us to trust the future to God and to recognize the new life that we are called to in the here and now. Our Judeo-Christian spirituality is one of both remembering and forgetting. We remember all of the great acts of salvation which God has performed in history, and we are assured of our security as children of God. But then is it important to forget the specifics of those redemptive acts because God is doing a new thing in our lives today.

While we tend to want to hang on to the traditions which help us remember, and repeat them over and over, God seeks to lead us forward into a newness which is authentically ours. We can remember the meaning of the past even as we create by God's grace the specifics for today.

There is an urgency in all of Jesus' teaching which compels us to let tomorrow take care of itself and attend to the matters of today in obedience to God's call to us. If we can do that we are living the kingdom of God, bringing heaven to earth, and are already enjoying what it means to be "raised with Christ." Surely this is what Jesus meant when he taught us to pray, "Thy kingdom come, thy will be done, on earth as it is in heaven."

Naturally, we hope our loved ones are in heaven and that we may see them again. We can commend them to the love of Christ and let go of our worry. Then with thankful hearts, we can attend to the business over which we have some real control, how we live our own lives.

If we truly understand what Easter and the Resurrection means, we will know it has as much to do with the quality of our lives now as in the future.

If Jesus was God incarnate,
where was God when Jesus walked upon the earth?

Your question invites an explanation of the Doctrine of the Holy Trinity. This doctrine is common to all historic Christian communities, and might be said to be the definitive test of Christian orthodoxy. Put simply, it describes our experience of one God in three ways, as creator, savior and sustainer. Through creation and God's interaction with creation, these three "faces" of God have been revealed. They are indivisible, yet often described as "persons."

While the validity of the Holy Trinity is based upon revelation rather than logic, we may get a sense of it by reflecting upon the various roles we play in our own lives. For example, you may be a parent, child and friend all at the same time, different persons to different people, yet the same human being. The doctrine of the Holy Trinity says that God has revealed to us what we need to know. The essence of our relationship with God is that God created us, saved us, and is present to help and invite us into an ever deepening friendship and appreciation of God's love for us.

The trinitarian doctrine does not define God. It does define our experience of God and reveal God to be trustworthy. It does not tell us everything there is to know about God. While we know what we need to know in order to give our hearts to God, we remember that God's greatness is beyond our knowing.

Preserving the mystery of God is critical to healthy Christian spirituality and interfaith relationships. For instance, when Christians encounter in other faiths the essential truths of the Holy Trinity beyond the historical events, we can affirm them because we know that God is greater than our description of our own experience of God.

Our spiritual lives grow into maturity through the three-fold experience of God. Essential to this process is a profound recognition of our limitations. In one way or another, we need to come to the awareness that we need God, that we are not God, and that we are really very small in the vastness of God's creation. This awareness may come from an encounter with nature, such as gazing into the night sky or feeling the thunder of waves at the ocean shore. It may also come when we "hit the wall" in some way, frustrated or devastated because our best efforts to find meaning have turned into ashes.

Also essential to our spiritual wholeness is knowing that we are deeply loved by God. These are the saving ways which God reaches out to us. It begins when we are held adoringly by our parents. As we look into their eyes, we intuitively know that we are precious. Later, a teacher may see our potential and inspire us. Still later, we experience mutual love.

In mid-life we may discover gifts which lay dormant within us from earlier years, and there is a burst of creativity. In our twilight years we often discover profound spiritual wholeness. These are just some of the ways God communicates salvation to us. Historically, God acted through people in revealing ways, and came to us once in a person, Jesus Christ, to love us firsthand and to complete our salvation.

One more ingredient is necessary to knowing the fullness of the Christian experience. It is the urge to follow. The ability to know the God who creates all there is and loves us as revealed in Jesus is a present reality not locked in the past. God experienced as Holy Spirit is God inviting us to be led into truth and ministry with the power of Christ's love in the here and now. This response to God's call is called faith; it is entrusting our lives to God, also called salvation. Conversion, however, is a lifelong process of spiritual maturation giving the theological term, sanctification. As Jesus promised, the Holy Spirit leads us into all truth.

The Doctrine of the Holy Trinity describes our experience of God, preserves the mystery of God, and provides the unity necessary to convey the faith to future generations. Where was God when Jesus walked upon the earth? The power of the Gospel is that when Jesus died for us, that sacrifice was offered by none other than the God who created all things and is present with us even today.

> *I was in the elevator the other day when someone asked me, "Are you saved?" I'm Roman Catholic, and found myself stumbling for an answer. I love the Lord and try to be a good Christian, but I felt defensive and unprepared with an answer. What would you have said?*

The best answer for that question is a simple, "Yes, thank you." Even if I were Jewish I would answer that way. People who ask that question are trained to counter almost any response you will come up with, because in their minds you are not part of their club until you go through their prescribed "right of passage."

Christianity is a missionary movement. Christian theology proclaims that humanity is unable to be at one with God without God's will and action to make it so. God is perceived through history as reaching out to humanity in order to establish an appropriate relationship with God which allows human beings to be truly blessed and to be a blessing to God's creation.

The supreme action of God in Christian history is the Christ event, when God came to us in our humanity in the person of Jesus Christ, in a sense, bringing heaven to earth. This is known as the saving event, and human beings could not be reconciled to God without it. With God's action, we are saved; without it, we are lost.

The action of God in Christ is a loving gift which liberates humanity from concern about God's love for all of us. Christians are called to share this good news, but ironically we often communicate the idea that God loves only those who are Christians. Some self-described Christians believe that salvation is available only through their particular sect.

How do we lose sight of God's unconditional love? Well, love must be received in order to be experienced, and this fact opens the door to placing conditions upon God's gift. Protestant Christianity has tended to stress the acceptance of God's love as the moment of salvation, while Catholic Christianity has tended to stress the giving of that love as the critical factor.

Once the emphasis on the reception of God's love becomes more important than the giving, the door is open to all kinds of distortions, and Protestant Christianity is noted for its historical and continuing disintegration. There are unlimited possibilities for the manner in which grace is received, and any one of them can be built into a church by leaders seeking to gain a following.

Salvation is a very complex experience. Consider the sacrament of baptism. Christians who baptize babies believe that Christ's love becomes meaningful for children through the community of believers who pledge to love them in Christ. Children may not understand their experiences rationally, but they know when they are loved and when they are not.

As children mature, it is important for them to make their own decisions about God, of course, but in the Catholic view, one does not need to wait to the age of reason to enjoy the full privileges of being a Christian. Nor is there a certain level of maturity which guarantees that we have appropriated God's grace fully.

Christians who baptize only adults or young adults believe that one must make the mature decision for Christ personally in order to be saved. No one can be a Christian for us; we must accept Christ and reject evil for ourselves. They tend to be acutely aware of the moment which they accepted Christ, while people who grew up as baptized Christians may not be aware of such a dramatic experience.

What both experiences of salvation share, ideally, is a deep sense of gratitude for the unconditional love of God known daily through a vital relationship with Jesus Christ as Lord and Savior. Such love bears the fruit of peace and joy and equips them to love others, not from needful emptiness which exploits, but from wholeness and the desire to give.

Rather than asking if others are saved, Christians would do better to remember that it is God who saves us all and charges us to help others to understand this through unconditional love. Jesus never asked anyone if they were saved, but he did say with word and deed, in effect "How can I help you?"

*You once stated "unequivo-
cally" that a woman's deceased father was in heaven
although he had not accepted Jesus as his Savior. But
the church has always taught that the salvation of Jesus
has no effect unless it is embraced by the individual.
The criteria to receive the benefits is belief. How can
you say otherwise?*

You are right that the traditional teaching of Christianity is that salvation must be believed to be effective. You refer to many scriptural passages to support this teaching and I will pass two of them on to readers. John's Gospel reports in 3:18 that Jesus said, "He who does not believe (in the Son) has been judged." And St. Paul said in Romans 8:1, "There is no condemnation for those who are in Christ Jesus."

These statements are indeed the Word of God. However, they are not justification for Christians to feel that they have an exclusive option on salvation. On the contrary, the love of God experienced in Christ Jesus demands that no conditions are placed upon the gift of salvation, and that inheritors of the kingdom are known by their fruit, not by doctrinal identity.

While Christians often seek to emulate the exclusiveness of the leaders of Jesus' own worshipping community, Jesus teaches a more inclusive way.

Luke records in his Gospel an incident where a lawyer (presumably a religious leader) asked Jesus this question: "Teacher, what must I do to inherit eternal life?" Jesus asked him if he knew God's law, and he correctly replied by referring to the Summary of the Law, to love God and your neighbor as yourself. Then he asked Jesus, "Who is my neighbor?" Jesus' response was to tell the story of the Good Samaritan.

You know the story. It's a familiar parable although recorded only in Luke' Gospel. Luke's focus was, in part, to communicate the universal consequences of the Christ event. Those who were considered to be believers did not help an injured man, avoiding him by crossing to the other side of the road. But a Samaritan, not a believer in the eyes of Jesus' community, did help the man, and therefore manifested obedience to the law.

In the Parable of the Good Samaritan Jesus himself defines what a believer is: One who loves the neighbor and places no restrictions upon the definition of neighbor. The Samaritan was not considered a child of God by the religious of Jesus' day. In fact, he would have been perceived to be despised by God. To Jesus, however, he was an inheritor of eternal life.

Jesus is the way, the truth and the life because he is the incarnate presence of the love of God. Christians hold this as our doctrine, yet we often exclude from fellowship and inheritance those who are filled with the love of God. To do so is to step outside of that love ourselves.

In Matthew's Gospel, it is reported that Jesus said, "Not everyone who says to me 'Lord, Lord,' shall enter the kingdom of heaven, but only the one who does the will of my Father in heaven." This admonishes Christians not to think that we can claim salvation simply by using the name of Jesus. The fruit of the Spirit - love - is the litmus test, as in the Good Samaritan story.

You will remember that the woman who asked the question to which you refer described her father as a very loving man. Sadly, he would not have qualified as a member of her particular church. But that is not the criterion of inheriting the Kingdom, so Jesus teaches us. If we wish to follow Jesus, we must accept his teaching in this matter.

Even though her father was a loving man, therefore already enjoying eternal life in this world, he would still need the forgiveness of God in Christ to ultimately receive the fullness of God's inheritance, just as you and I do. That's why Christians have always said that Christ is the only way.

I've never understood what Jesus meant in Mark's Gospel when he said there is only one unforgivable sin, the sin against the Holy Spirit. What does it mean to sin against the Holy Spirit?

To understand the unforgivable sin, it is helpful to think of the nature of gifts. When you are offered a gift, it is necessary for you to receive it some way in order to enjoy it. You reach out and take it, you unwrap it, perhaps, and then you use it. If you reject the gift, then it cannot accomplish what was intended. While it has its own intrinsic value, the gift's potential value and true purpose is left unrealized.

To reject the gift of God's forgiveness is the sin against the Holy Spirit. It is unforgivable because the nature of forgiveness is reciprocal. Like all gifts, it must be received in order to be effective.

Mark's Gospel offers a clue to the nature of the sin against the Holy Spirit by telling us that Jesus spoke about it after he had taught about forgiveness and consequently began to incur the wrath of the religious authorities. In fact, they accused him of being in league with Beelzebub, or Satan. They not only considered his teaching undesirable, but evil. It violated their sense of right and wrong. In the midst of this controversy in the third chapter of Mark, Jesus cautions, "All sins will be forgiven people, and whatever blasphemes they utter; but whoever blasphemes against the Holy Spirit never has forgiveness, but is guilty of an eternal sin."

Jesus began by saying that God's forgiveness is greater than any sin we might commit. His words from the cross, "Father, forgive them, for they know not what they do" indicate the radical extent of God's forgiveness. This is, in part, the reason Jesus was rejected by so many. Unlimited forgiveness is unacceptable by worldly standards. Yes, we can understand God forgiving some sins, or the sins of some people. But we feel the line must be drawn somewhere. We cannot accept, for example, that God would forgive an Adolf Hitler or that we should be expected to.

Forgiveness, however, is God's gift offered to all and it has no conditions or limitations. Taking the initiative, God extends the healing and renewing possibilities of a fresh start for all of us.

Yet, not all of us accept the gift. We are free to consider God's forgiveness undesirable. And we do. Perhaps it is more accurate to say that all of us reject the grace of God to some degree. It is like trying to look into a bright light; we must turn away, at least partially, because it is too much for us. God's forgiveness violates our sense of justice and order. We want wrongs to be punished, not forgiven. Most of us can accept God's forgiveness for ourselves, but we cannot understand how God can forgive others. Some of us cannot grasp God's acceptance even of ourselves.

The sin against the Holy Spirit then is not something we do, but the limitation we all have in receiving the grace of God. We all sin against the Holy Spirit to the degree that we are unable to receive and to give forgiveness.

The inability to receive forgiveness, while present in all of us to some degree, can be minimized through faith. The ability to forgive comes when we make the conscious decision to forgive even when the feeling may not yet be present. It may be impossible for us, but it is not impossible for Christ acting through us. Accepting the idea that we are acceptable to God is the beginning. After that, it is simply a matter of being conduits for the mercy of God acting through us.

No one should worry that something done may be unforgivable. But we might all ask ourselves if we are truly sorry for the wrongs we do and the rights we leave undone. Heartfelt repentance is the appropriate response to God's forgiveness. The sin against the Holy Spirit is saying "No, thank you" to God.

I've always been confused over the "mixed message" of Christianity. We're told to "love your neighbor as yourself," but we're also told by Jesus in Luke 14:26 that we must hate our very selves in order to be his followers. Would you discuss this?

The essential message of the Christian faith is that each of us is cherished by God. Certainly none of us is perfect in our actions, and it would be reasonable to expect that God is unhappy with us individually and collectively for the way we treat creation and one another. God has a right to be angry. The cross of Christ tells us that while God is terribly hurt by humanity's behavior, God's love is constant and ever-ready to find expression through a mutual, loving and active relationship. Forgiveness overrides God's right to be angry.

If God loves us so much, then we must conclude that we are lovable and love ourselves. We may also conclude that others are lovable and try to love them. Faith leads believers to become messengers. Once we know the nature of God's love for us, we realize that we have no basis for withholding ourselves.

To hate "self" in the sense in which Jesus speaks is to turn away from the perception that being human is at the center of the universe. The ego learns this from the world. The world provides instant reward when we please and punishment when we don't. People try to make us into what they want us to be, and we learn early to cooperate. Of course, this leads to pain because the self which is formed through this process is not created from within. When others mold us, our identity becomes enmeshed with theirs. In turn, we can become unable to understand and appreciate those different from our own culture.

When the Bible teaches us to love others as ourselves, it invites us to see the same beauty in our humanity which God sees. It is allowing God to be the greatest influence in our lives rather than the world around us. Jesus came to reveal the truth about humanity, that we are loved, in contrast to the false truth which the world gives, that we are unlovable unless we do something to deserve it.

The struggle of Jesus in the wilderness with the devil was all about being tempted to prove his identity. Satan said, in effect, "If you are really loved by God, then jump off of this building and God will send angels to catch you." The temptation is to create situations which prove we are lovable. For instance, if we've had a nurturing childhood, the temptation is to be hooked on others' affection. If we haven't, the temptation is to defy the affection of others as though to say, "I'll show you!"

There is a difference between loving ourselves and being in love with ourselves. The former is the knowledge that we are wonderful because God made us and loves us. The latter is the false idea that we are wonderful because of how we look or what we have accomplished in our lives.

We tend to react emotionally to others' expectations of us, and feel unaccepted if we cannot or choose not to meet them. If we love ourselves, however, because we know that God loves us, we are able to respond to peoples' needs with reasonable communication rather than emotional reactions, or by distancing ourselves from them. To respond rather than to react is one of the signs of a person who knows the love of God, is secure in that love, and is free to simply be and let be.

There is no mixed message in Christianity. It is very clear that our mission is to allow God's love and nothing else to mold our character and actions.

I'm always amused when I hear people give credit to God for saving them from some kind of disaster because I never hear anyone blaming God when others are not saved. Don't you think God should be given credit for both good and bad?

Your question raises the issue of grace. What, exactly, is the nature of God's relationship with humanity? Did God set creation going and then sit back to see what happens? Or, is God continuing to be involved in the creative process? Most people of faith would hold the latter, while the degree of involvement might be argued.

Accidents happen, and while God might be blamed for creating a world in which accidents can happen, few would stretch that so far as to say that God caused the accident. On the other hand, God gives us the grace to respond to accidents in life-giving ways by learning from them, and growing in our appreciation of the gift of life.

God gives us the freedom to make choices and to be partners with God in the ongoing process of creation. Choices lead to situations in which people are going to get hurt. We can appreciate feelings of gratitude when saved from a disaster. We can also appreciate that people's lives can be profoundly changed under such circumstances. Those who are lost in accidents are grieved for, and those who survive often experience a sense that they must "do something" with the gift they have been given. It is in this sense that God can be thanked for the fact that a life was accidentally spared. (Tragically, we sometimes learn just how much we value loved ones only by losing them.)

Faith's view is larger than the material world. Because of God's love we know that there is hope beyond physical death. We know that God is on the side of those who are victimized, that God loves sinners as well as the righteous, and that God has promised to be with us always. While we grieve at any loss of human life, we also place our trust in the very real experience that there is more to creation than its physical manifestations. In essence, what God has instilled in our hearts is even more important than what God has planted in our minds.

People are hurt not only by accidents, but also by intent. When we consciously set out to serve ourselves at the expense of others, we certainly cannot blame God. Much of human misery in the world is the result of conscious human behavior devoid of empathy for others. This is the essence of sin, and it is the antithesis of God's call to us.

The circumstances of our lives are not nearly as important as how we respond to them. The blessing of wealth, for example, can be used to hurt others or to help them. The same is true of technology, or education, or natural talents. While some might say, "Look what God has done to this person compared to that one," a faith perspective would say, "Look what this person has done with the life which has been given him."

It is not a matter of blaming God or giving God credit. Rather, it is a question of recognizing that we have choices to make and these choices work for good or evil.

There's been a lot of passionate dialogue in our newspaper between atheists and believers on whether God exists. I would like to know what convinced you of God's existence.

Because human beings are not omniscient, we have to make a choice to be a believer or a nonbeliever. No one can be absolutely certain about the existence of God. We need to be humble on both sides of the argument. The dogmatism of the atheist is just as blind as the dogmatism of rigid faith positions.

I conclude that God exists from my experiences and the experiences of many I trust, not to mention the vast majority of human beings through history. My life is molded (when I'm at my best) by the God I know through the Judeo-Christian tradition and particularly my own relationship with Jesus Christ. I may be wrong, but I cannot betray what I have found to be true.

To love God and one another is to be truly alive. This is the proclamation of the Christ event, and I know of no superior truth. I also know that further absolutes only divide the human family. In his great treatise on God's love in 1 Corinthians 13, St. Paul cautioned us not to let any absolutes other than the unconditional love of God rule our lives.

Like Paul, we all see in a mirror dimly and know only in part. Apart from loving the way God loves us, we cannot make excessive claims to truth. Beyond love, absolutes are for the foolish.

The quest for knowledge of God moves forward on two levels. One is to know about God, the other to simply know God. We can relate this to any friendship. There are many things we can know about someone without knowing them personally. Conversely, we can know someone pretty well, or think we do, without having much information about them.

Reason, philosophy, logic and empirical evidence are the tools for knowing about God. The debates are usually lively with good arguments on either side, but ultimately from a rational point of view alone God can neither be proven to exist nor proven not to exist. One rational argument, for example, might be that God does not exist (in any meaningful way for us, at least) because God cannot be experienced through the senses. God cannot be observed.

To this, one might present the argument that the evident experience of God in a great variety of ways from the earliest moment of human existence constitutes empirical evidence. Scientists know of the existence of heavenly objects with near certainty while not being able to see them by the influence they have upon other objects. Can we not then rationally conclude that God exists because of the influence of God or gods claimed by the vast majority of human beings throughout history? To this, there is a perfectly rational response, and the debate goes on and on.

The debate above is of little concern, however, to those who know God in a personal way. We may not be able to fully understand our experiences, but we cannot discount them simply because they cannot be weighed and measured. Perhaps if no one else in the world had such experiences, we might be insane, but instead we find that encounters with God in one form or another (even if in rejection) are part of what defines us as human beings.

Just as knowledge about God has its tools, so does knowing

God personally. It begins with faith, taking that leap of trusting even when we don't have the empirical evidence. Once we have crossed that barrier which we ourselves have built, we are in a new world. We also have new tools. We don't have to leave behind the tools of reason and empirical evidence, but these are supplemented by prayer, worship, service and the fellowship and wisdom of the faith community.

Even if we could know everything there is to know about God, we would still have to make the decision to become God's friend, to give our heart as well as our mind. Friendship is always a two-way street. When an early cosmonaut returned from circling the earth he contributed to Soviet propaganda by stating, "I have been to heaven and there was no God there."

In response, a Russian Orthodox priest said, "If you cannot see God on Earth, you will never see God in heaven."

Jesus is usually pictured by artists as meek and mild, kind of a milquetoast. I find it difficult to see that kind of person as the savior of the world. What do you think he was really like?

J esus may be portrayed as you describe in the artist's efforts to represent him as being unlike our expectations. The world expects a savior to be a Schwarzenegger type. Worldly powers rely on the likes of wealth, physical strength and political power. But God's strength is not a matter of being greater, but of a different nature completely. God's ways are not our ways, the Bible tells us. God's power is the power of love.

It may also be said that while Jesus was physically male, his personality serves as a model for both male and female. He embodied the best of our humanity, incorporating both the feminine and masculine traits which lead to wholeness of life. Perhaps the effort to express both his masculine and feminine traits artistically has led to the "milquetoast" portrayal you mention.

The remarkable proclamation of the Gospel is the incarnation. God became a human being, and while Jesus is therefore the expected Messiah, he is also someone you and I can identify with. Or, to reverse that, he can identify with you and me, and therefore is truly "God with us."

As Messiah, he stirred peoples' relationship with God. While threatening many by establishing an untraditional and forgiving value system, he refreshed others because he offered them hope and the assurance of belonging to God's kingdom. Everyone had a decision to make: Do I follow him or not?

It was difficult for many to follow him because he was too normal in his humanity. He was known to those in his home town as just another kid. He didn't fit their preconceived notions of a savior in his lifestyle or his teaching. He spoke of acceptance, servanthood and sacrifice, while he lived these values in his own life. While he performed miracles, he cautioned people not to be impressed by them alone, but by God's message of forgiveness.

The issue of the Christian message is found in the union between God and humanity in Jesus. Can one accept it? Can we accept a God who came to be with us fully, but didn't clean up the mess we are in? Can we accept a God who cried and cooed as a child, wet his diapers, went through the terrible twos and sassed his parents? Can we accept a God who entered the experience of growing and learning, and in the process irritated the neighbors, had a fist fight or two, knew the urgency of sexual attraction and the quickening of his mind through education?

It may be hard for us to think of God in these ways, but when we do we realize that such a God is with us in the full force of human experience, its joys and its sorrows, its loneliness and passions, its anxieties and uncertainties. Jesus was not above these realities.

No, I don't think Jesus was meek in the usual sense of the word. He faced the real stuff of life we do, and he showed us how to do that in the love of God.

I quit going to church because it was so negative. It seemed like it was always the same message: human beings are sinners and the world is going to hell in a handbasket. Instead of feeling better, I always felt worse after church. Why are Christians such negative thinkers?

The good news in Jesus Christ is that God forgives us and accepts us. The church's duty is to proclaim forgiveness and break through the reality of sin.

To be open to God's forgiveness one must feel a profound need for it. Therefore, to be successful in proclaiming God's forgiveness of sin the church must also succeed in pointing out the sin. While this may feel negative, it is the beginning of hope and the expression of love.

When I leave the house in the morning, I hope that my wife will mention it if my clothes don't match or I've forgotten something. Because she loves me, I don't consider this input negative. Friends trust one another enough to offer constructive criticism. On a more serious level, the church's call to repentance should be honored.

The image of Jesus on the cross is an acute reminder of the consequences of our sinful thoughts and actions. But, because of Jesus' words from the cross we know that God is forgiving. When we contemplate the suffering now of people in the world around us, we can either deny our own involvement, like Peter, or we can admit our complicity and ask God to help us change our ways.

Sin is a break with God. It is the presence in our hearts, souls, and minds of an attitude which separates us from God. Perhaps on top of the list is pride, when we think we have all of the answers and when we are not open to what God has to teach us. Though Christians are quick to attribute pride to unbelievers, it is common within communities of faith.

In fact, when unbelievers refuse to accept the premise of faith, I often find what they really reject is the closed-mindedness of so many faith communities and our nasty habit of judging others while ignoring our own behavior.

48

We as believers tend to project as whole truth the little bit garnered from our life's experiences and religious tradition. But our perspective doesn't make others wrong. Rather, different perspectives held together offer dimensions of God's revelation we would not otherwise see. Getting a fix on truth requires more than one angle. All good navigators know this.

Another attitude which separates us from God is lust, the sin of exploitation. Usually wrongly associated with sexual desire, lust is relating to others and the world as ours to enjoy without regard for them, the common good or the purpose of God. The opposite of lust is love, the commitment to nurture others by contributing to their welfare, not simply using them for our own pleasure. In the long run, of course, we are blessed when we learn how to love.

Related to lust is gluttony, a lack of appreciation for the blessings of God's creation. It is when we mindlessly consume God's gifts, grabbing what we can get with no thought for taking only what we need. Too often a full stomach or a fat checking account becomes a substitute for a grateful heart. For example, stuffing oneself with food indicates a spiritually unhealthy way to try to satisfy a hunger which has nothing to do with food. Twelve-step programs remind us that recovery from these kinds of addictions begins by admitting our helplessness and turning to a meaningful relationship with God, or a Higher Power, if you prefer. This is repentance. Such turning is appropriate as a gift of ourselves to God in trust, gratitude, and commitment.

Catholic tradition lists seven mortal sins, including the three above, while Protestants have tended not to divide sins into greater or lesser categories. Anything which separates us from God is a sin. If our lives are sincerely oriented toward God, we will not be perfect, but we will grow in faith and fruitfulness. The church has a loving duty to call our attention to the ways we stray from God's path.

You said in a column that God strengthens us to embrace the hard times. But how can I release the hurt I feel when I see the pain and suffering around me? Shortly after my husband's death I learned of my daughter's cancer, which has left her physically devastated, even if she now goes into remission. I have friends whose problems are as bad, not to mention what I read in the newspapers. My question is this: How can I release the hurt I feel?

To feel the burden of others' suffering is one of God's gifts to us. It is, of course, not the kind of gift which makes us feel good. Yet, without the ability to empathize with others when they suffer, we would not be expressing our humanity fully. Nor would we be walking the pilgrimage of faith: compassion.

For Christians and all people of faith, compassion is the beginning. The Gospel of Mark reveals the heart of God when Jesus looks upon the crowd. "He had compassion for them because they were like sheep without a shepherd." Then he taught them and fed them in what is known as the miracle of the loaves and fishes.

The Incarnation is the belief that God acted from compassion to be present with us, to suffer with us, and to redeem our suffering. As Hebrews 4:15 reminds us, "We do not have a high priest who is unable to sympathize with our weaknesses, but we have one who in every respect has been tested as we are, yet without sin." Faith begins with the knowledge that in the midst of our questions and trials, when we long for answers and release, God's heart goes out to us.

Faith is the human response to a compassionate God. We will never have all the answers, and we will never be free from trials in this world, but what we have is better: the grace of God to respond when our own hearts resonate with the suffering of others.

Therefore, we pray for release from hurt with mixed feelings, because hurt is an appropriate emotion when people are suffering. We don't pray to become callous. And we are not really praying for all suffering to go away because we know that it is part of life as

God has given it. We also do not pray that only those we love not suffer, with no regard for anyone else. What we really pray for is how to respond to the hurt we feel rather than our release from it.

Returning to the miracle of loaves and fishes, which I am citing from the sixth chapter of Mark's Gospel, the disciples were looking for an escape from the problem of the people's hunger when they suggested that Jesus send them home. But Jesus said to the disciples, "You give them something to eat." God's way expressed through Jesus was to take what was available, give thanks for it, break it, and share it. All ate and were filled.

Faith's response to the suffering of others is not to avoid it, but to take what one has to work with, give thanks to God for it, and put it into action.

Your question suggests that you are a person of compassion, and that is painful. But don't let go of it. Like Jesus, we will sometimes say the prayer, "Abba, Father, with you all things are possible; remove this cup from me." But we would also wish to be with Jesus as he finishes the prayer, "Yet, not what I want, but what you want." What God wants is for you to fulfill your ministry as Jesus fulfilled his. Your hurt is your connection to the heart of Jesus.

You will find when you give thanks for what you have to work with, that you will feel a new sense of strength and purpose. Discouragement is no match for the power of the Holy Spirit working through us to bring Christ's love into the world. You have unique gifts for healing and communicating the comfort and hope of God's love in the midst of suffering. You care, and that is the most important release of the power of those gifts. You are what Henri Nouwen has described as a "wounded healer," a term which captures the essence and power of Christian ministry.

When Jesus said to St. Paul, "My grace is sufficient for you," he was not offering him a consolation prize; rather, he was offering Paul the opportunity to be a means of grace through compassion because of his own suffering.

I am a Christian, yet I have
this feeling that I have lived before in previous lives.
Can a Christian believe in reincarnation?

Christians don't generally believe in reincarnation. There are several important reasons, based on the Christian theology of creation and grace.

Unlike traditions which believe the soul is eternal and has a pre-existence prior to human birth, Christians believe the whole person is created by God when born into this world. Body and soul are created inseparable. At the resurrection, a new spiritual body is given as the whole person is raised from the dead.

Life in this world has a beginning and an end. It is a precious gift. That is why our Judeo-Christian tradition stresses how important it is to use our lives well. We have an opportunity not only to experience life's blessings, but more importantly, to experience God. Biological life could be described as a window to our creator. The very personal nature of Jesus' ministry tells us that God cares about each one of us. We are created with the ability to know God and to enter the stream of God's love which gives meaning to all of creation. Jesus invites us to accept the Good News of God's desire to be in fellowship with us forever. All we have to do is say yes to that invitation.

I am describing grace. While we struggle in life to find our way, God is courting us. Life's events have a way of awakening our desire for God. Sometimes we are overwhelmed by the beauty and wonder of life.

Some may see God's invitation in the beautiful complexity of nature or the mystery of life. Others may experience that peace which passes understanding in times of great need. Even the dry times can be powerful times of spiritual growth, viewed in retrospect. Many come to God when faced with the realities of their own sinful actions.

Grace is God working in our lives to help us choose the path of love. Notice that the choice is ours; that's part of grace, too. No one is forced into a relationship with God, but it is an offer too great to refuse.

Grace collides with the idea of karma, the core of reincarnation theology. Karma is the idea that behavior in previous lives determines the nature of this life. In other words, reincarnation alleges that we are living the consequences of what we have done or left undone in previous incarnations of the soul. But God's forgiveness cancels the need for karma.

Our salvation does not depend upon our getting it right or paying the debt of previous indiscretions. Rather, it depends upon the fact that God loves us and accepts us without condition. We could not work our way into heaven in a million lifetimes. Yet, it is ours because of one human life whom Christians believe to be God incarnate, Jesus of Nazareth.

Many people experience what you describe as a previous life. There is so much we don't know about the human mind, that there are certainly other possible reasons for this common feeling. Perhaps it has to do with our subconscious, or even a collective subconscious reality which connects us with those who have gone before.

Since we all draw from the mind of God, there must be times when our intuitive connections tap into the past. Some, apparently, have even been able to look into the future with amazing accuracy.

When we say we "believe in" something, we not only mean that it exists, but that we trust in it. To believe in reincarnation is therefore to trust not in the grace of God, but in the ability of the soul to redeem itself. While we may be fascinated with the idea of reincarnation, we would not want to stake our lives on it. Better to trust in God's unconditional love.

You almost never mention the judgment of God. Is there no room for judgment in your theology?

Your question strikes at the very core of Christian theology. How we view the judgment of God determines, to a great extent, how we view ourselves and one another.

It must be said at first that God is our judge. This is simply to say that God has a purpose in creation, a purpose for our lives, and that only God knows the degree to which we are living in accord with those intentions. Since none of us as human beings has the perspective which God has, no one is worthy of judging another. This is true despite the insights we are able to garner from life's experiences and God's revelation to us through our religious traditions.

Even our secular system acknowledges that motive and innate ability are factors in the accountability of our actions. We cannot know the factors leading to another's actions which may on the surface seem easily evaluated. Furthermore, we are incapable of stepping outside of our own prejudices to impartially judge another person. We all too easily see the sliver in the eye of another while ignoring the log in our own eye, as Jesus said. For all of these reasons, Jesus encourages us to let God do the judging.

To say that God is our judge is to place the emphasis upon the word "God" rather than upon the word "judge." The perspective from which God judges us and the way in which we are judged is revealed in the life and ministry of Jesus. It is so radically different from the way the world judges, and from the religious sense of judgment which Jesus encountered from those who sought God's acceptance through obedience to the law, that the word "judge" needs to maintain the quotation marks.

God's judgment must be seen in the context of Jesus' love. This is the heart of the Good News. Imagine yourself guilty of a crime which, according to society, deserves the death penalty. There you are in the courtroom with your attorney, the one who is bound to fight for your acquittal, and at the other end of the table is your accuser, the one bound to convict you and fight for your execution.

You have no idea what the outcome will be, and you are naturally afraid for your life. Suddenly the judge appoints your defense attorney to take the bench and make the final decision. Of course, your attorney will acquit you because that is what he is committed to do.

This is the essence of Christian theology and doctrine: The judge is actually our defense attorney. Remember the words of St. John, "But if anyone does sin, we have an advocate with the Father, Jesus Christ the righteous, and he is the atoning sacrifice for our sins, and not for ours only but also for the sins of the whole world." (I John 2:1)

If Jesus' life acquits us in the eyes of God, then what of justice? Is it right simply to forgive and never to hold accountable? Of course not. But once justice is viewed from the perspective of Jesus' love, the driving force is restoration, not punishment. The goal is to reconcile an offender with God and with those who have been offended.

The means toward that end has to do with a community's involvement in bringing the offender to a sense of responsibility for what has happened, to right the wrong, if possible, to rehabilitate and restore to fellowship. It is also the goal of restorative justice to help victims to be healed, to replace their confidence in the community, and to lessen their fears in the future.

If we think of judgment as the process of separating the good from the bad, then we are working at cross purposes with God who loves us all. But if we think of judgment as knowing those times when the community is broken, when someone has lost his way, and we must work to find them and restore them to the fold, then we are judging as Jesus judges us.

BIBLICAL
INSPIRATION

*If the Bible is the inspired word of God, why
are there so many contradictions in the different Gospel stories about Jesus? Is God contradicting himself?*

It is true that there are contradictions in the historical details of
the Gospel stories, but people of faith should not be concerned
by this. In fact, the varied way in which the stories are told provides a rich tapestry for spiritual understanding.

Before addressing your question specifically, let me offer a
little more background on how the Gospels evolved. From eyewitness accounts an oral tradition developed about Jesus. Eventually, some 30 or 40 years after Jesus was crucified, these stories
were collected, edited and written in the first Gospel.

Most scholars believe that the first written Gospel was Mark,
although there is strong evidence that there was another Gospel
contemporary to or older than Mark because Matthew and Luke
seem to have it as a source apart from Mark. The Gospel of John
seems to draw largely from an entirely independent tradition, while
John was almost certainly aware of Mark, Matthew, and Luke.

While oral tradition was more reliable in a largely illiterate
society, there is no question that over time stories were modified
through error. Anyone who's ever played the game of whispering
something to a person next to you and having the information go
around a circle as though a secret were being told, knows how the
message changes from beginning to end. Imagine this phenomenon taking place over a period of decades.

One cause, then, for contradictions in the Gospel stories is that mistakes were made and compounded through the storytelling. But a far greater reason for contradictions was the practice of altering a story in order to relate its spiritual meaning. We must realize that people of Jesus' time lived in a religious age, not a scientific age. Therefore, story-telling was not the scientific truth, but the religious truth revealed in history. This was particularly so for the Gospels, whose purpose was to impart revelation from God by telling the story of Jesus.

The Gospel stories of Jesus were almost certainly altered to address the historical situation of the early followers of Jesus. As the stories were told in varied Christian communities, the common stories took on a variety of expressions. Mark was writing to an essentially Gentile Christian community, and was concerned with stressing the centrality of servanthood in the message of Jesus and the life of the Church.

The Gospel of Matthew was written for Jewish Christians struggling to cope with separation from their Jewish roots and community. Luke addressed some of the issues which came later in the early Church, such as the delayed return of Jesus, the beginnings of persecutions of the Church from Roman authorities, and the increasing hostility between Jewish and Gentile Christians.

The Book of John is generally believed to have come later than the other three and challenges early Christian ideas which were not considered to be of the "true faith." One of these, for example, stated that Jesus was divine, but only "appeared" to be human.

Believers need not be shaken by biblical authors' alterations. The inspiration of the Bible does not lie in its complete historical accuracy, but in the belief that the history is told through the inspiration of the Holy Spirit. In other words, if Jesus is quoted, whether he said the exact words historically or whether he said them as Risen Lord by inspiring the evangelist, the words still belong to Jesus.

The task of people of faith is to allow the Holy Spirit to inspire us as we meditate upon the biblical stories and lessons. Where there are contradictions, we are less concerned with reconciling the disparity than with appreciating the lessons contained in the diversity.

We can see how the Holy Spirit applied the truth of Christ's love to the varied historical situations of the early Church. Our task as believers is to apply the truths of the Gospel to the history of our own lives. In this sense, we are still writing the Gospel.

Would you please write about the grace of God and Jesus Christ, what it is and what it means in people's lives?

G race is the foundation of faith revealed in Judeo-Christian tradition. Briefly, grace can be said to be God's love made manifest in creation, especially between God and humanity. Many verses of the Bible, both Hebrew and Greek, summarize the nature of grace. Most familiar to Christians is John 3:16: "For God so loved the world that he gave his only Son, so that everyone who believes in him may not perish but may have eternal life." Let's take a closer look at this verse.

"For God so loved the world," means God's love is unconditional in character, i.e., it is not earned, but given freely. A response to God's initiative is called forth, but is not a prerequisite for love. Grace gives us the freedom to choose how to respond. We can take God's love seriously, we can ignore God, or we can reject God. We may do all three at stages in life, but through it all, God's love is constant.

Grace allows the experience of God to unfold freely within certain parameters. Love embraces the freedom to hurt one another, for example. Ironically, hurting is part of learning how to love. God uses the lessons of life to teach, constantly inviting us into a more meaningful relationship, but giving us our rope. Through trial and error, hurt and forgiveness, sorrow and rebirth, we mature spiritually.

In theological terms, this is the process of sin, repentance, and redemption. We do not return to a holier state; rather, we move forward into the holiness of God made possible through sin and redemption.

"..that he gave his only begotten Son.." This phrase does not mean that God sent someone else, but that God came personally to be with us fully in our humanity. This is the mystery of the incar-

61

nation, another parameter of grace. It is a mystery not in the sense that it is incomprehensible, but in the sense that our ability to comprehend expands through growing intimacy with God. Because God "limits" what it is to be God in order to dwell with us in what it is to be human, we can know God in a very personal way. This is God's gift to us.

Christians experience in Jesus Christ a God who loves us always, even beyond the grave, and longs to receive our love in return.

The crucifixion and resurrection are the focal points of Christianity. Jesus' words from the cross teach us God's response to sin: "Father, forgive them for they know not what they do." God pays a great price for our actions, but the resurrection proves that the love of God is still with us to help us move forward with renewed power and perspective.

"...that all who believe in him would not perish but have eternal life." Eternal life is the goal of faith. It is a quality of life which feels reconciled with the creator and with creation. It trusts God's presence and power to redeem all that we encounter, to make a difference in our lives and our world, and to last beyond this life into a future more wonderful than we can imagine. Eternal life is not a quantity of time so much as a quality of existence which grows in the love of God. Faith is our response to the grace of God.

In a recent column you stated that the Biblical story of the Hebrew people conquering the Holy Land contained the inspired message of God within the uninspired context of history. I find this confusing. How do you know what is inspired and what isn't?

If we say that the Bible is the inspired word of God, do we mean that God dictated every word? Do we mean that we are intended to take every word literally, to view every event as having happened exactly as it is recorded? While many people of faith view the Bible in this way, most do not. Divine inspiration is more subtle than that.

When the Church proclaimed the Bible as the Word of God, it

certified that the Bible contains everything we need to know for salvation. God's truth is contained therein. The Bible is the standard against which all other ideas and perspectives are measured. The standard is not contained in the historical circumstances of the stories themselves, but in the truth which God reveals through the history.

Our task, then, is to hear God speaking in history through the Bible, not so we can replicate that history, but so we can hear God speaking today.

The Bible is the recorded history of people coming to faith over a long period of time in many places. In its pages we see faith evolve as the dynamic between God and the people of the Judeo-Christian tradition. Through their interpretation of events, their struggles to learn how to live faithfully together, their successes and their failures, we learn how God uses our lives to reveal true life to us. God engages with us in history, seeks to connect with us in meaningful ways, and provides minds and hearts to ponder the great mysteries of life and death, of love and hate, of good and evil. In the Bible we find God inviting humanity into a fellowship which imbues the material world with eternal meaning and causes us to hope beyond the limits of our transitory lives.

How does one discern God's truth revealed in the stories based upon the historical events? It's not an absolute process, but there are some well-tested guidelines to follow. First, consider the whole Bible rather than isolated parts of it. Certainly meditation upon any given part of scripture can bring great rewards, but each part must be weighed in the light of the full revelation contained therein. This is why it is wise to become well-versed in all of scripture and not build your theology upon only a few verses, or even books, of the Bible.

Having said that, however, there are parts of the Bible which must be given more importance than others. Certainly for Christians the words of Jesus in the four Gospels are more important than the words of any one prophet, or even of St. Paul. The prophet is important because his words help prepare the soil out of which the Christ experience grows. The apostle is important because he witnesses to his experience of Christ. But the experience itself is superior to preparing for it or witnessing to it. Jesus' words in the

Gospels allow us to see his Spirit in the rest of scripture as well. The Gospels also help us to see where parts of the Bible may be inconsistent with his teaching. (There is the question, of course, as to which words of Jesus are truly his and which are attributed to him by the Gospel writers through church tradition. In either case, the content of the Gospels is paramount for Christians.)

We also have the collective wisdom of our faith communities to guide us. It is important to humbly weigh our own perception of God's word against what Christians have taught over the centuries and what our own community teaches today. The great variety of ideas can be confusing. On the other hand, we know we have a great pool of living water from which to draw, the rich diversity of insight in the larger body of the faithful.

Finally, we have been given wonderful minds to reason and to imagine, and to pray. Ultimately, each person must wrestle with the great questions and apply the answers, imperfect though they may be, to one's own life. This is both a gift and a great responsibility.

It isn't enough to be told what is divinely inspired and what isn't, in the Bible or anywhere else. Ultimately, one must hear God's voice personally. The Bible is a tool of faith, not the object of faith. Your faith community and your God-given gifts of reason and intuition will help you to use the tool wisely and lovingly.

Could you offer some perspective on the old controversy of creation vs. evolution? Are these concepts mutually exclusive, or can the modern Christian be accepting of evolution?

Yes, many Christians are accepting of evolution. While this issue is usually expressed as a controversy between creation and evolution, the real controversy is between biblical literalists and the scientific community. Believe it or not, most Christians are not biblical literalists, and are quite able to integrate biblical faith with scientific theory.

The truth revealed in the Bible is not always revealed through literal interpretation. Some stories are intended to be accepted literally and others for the message they reveal in a nonhistorical way. The Book of Jonah, for example, is generally understood to be mythical in the best sense. While highly instructive of human spiritual reality, the story never really happened.

The creation stories — and one should be aware that there are two contrasting stories in the first and second chapters of Genesis — fall into the category of myth for many, if not most, Christians and Jews. The stories tell us truths about the multifaceted relationship between God and creation, particularly God's intention for humanity. But the stories tell us nothing scientific, hardly the concern of religious leaders in a pre-scientific age.

Of course, much of the Bible is history, and has been proven by archaeology to be generally correct where it is historical. Disciplined Bible study is always concerned in part with what may be actual history and what may be the storytellers' interpretive work. Both contain God's truth. If we can discern between history and interpretation, more of the truth unfolds.

This question is almost always addressed from the religious community's perspective, but it must also be said that many in the scientific community are also people of deep religious convictions. Science is not antithetical to faith. For people of faith, the application of the disciplines of the mind to natural reality is one of the ways God's truths are revealed to humanity. Certainly a profound sense of wonder is the beginning of scientific inquiry. We need not polarize faith and science, but integrate them.

Ironically, the man who started the evolution controversy was himself both a Christian and a scientist. Charles Darwin was a 19th century student of theology called early in life to ordination in the Church of England. Although ordination was not to be, he never felt that his theories regarding evolution were contrary to the Bible or the teachings of the Church. He was driven, however, in his later life to become an agnostic because of antagonistic pressure from the literalists of his own time.

Christians should be the last of faithful people to condemn scientific theories such as evolution. The Incarnation, central to our faith, affirms the goodness of the natural world and its usefulness as a means of grace. We should be concerned when scientific theory begins to make claims beyond its boundaries, as when a science is used to disprove the existence of God. But within its capabilities, science is instructive to the faithful. And, when the faithful embrace science, they acquire the power to speak to the modern scientific world.

I want to know how the loving and just God of your Bible can permit the horrors we see daily around the world and the many private horrors we never see that go on behind so many closed doors, and then expect us to accept his grace and reality?

Your question reveals your compassion for others. From my perspective, your pain as you reflect upon the horrors which are very real in the world places you very close to the heart of God. If God exists as the loving God we experience in Jesus, then the suffering of God is unimaginable as human beings suffer at the hands of one another. And much of the abuse and violence is done in the very name of God!

One possible conclusion is that God does not exist. Your question, however, demands a response from the other possibility. If God exists and is a loving God, why do these things happen?

One response is to say that we have no right to judge God. We might call this the Job response. The Book of Job portrays your question in an extended story of the suffering of a good man. The real power of the story lies in Job's struggle to be faithful even when events defy reasonable faith. To put it simply, it's easy to believe in God when everything feels good and fits our idea of the way life ought to be. It's hard to believe in God when life does not go our way or fit our sense of justice. The story confronts the notion that God ought to reward those who are good and punish those who are bad. Job is rewarded in the end, but that part of the story is generally considered to be a later addition which sells out to the popular way of thinking.

The point of Job is that we struggle with a God who does not play by our rules. Faith is not simply a matter of accepting what we cannot fully explain, however. God has revealed more to us.

Part of the gift of creation is its mortality. Without the reality of death and the pain and suffering which is naturally associated with it, physically and emotionally, one wonders whether life would be precious. Certainly our mortality stimulates a longing for the non-material aspects of life, an interest in spiritual things which Jesus describes as the treasures of heaven. Much of what we ascribe to evil may be, and probably is from God's perspective, a blessing - God's invitation to let go of dependence upon creation and trust in the creator.

Another part of the gift of creation is our ability to make choices. God has given us the freedom to choose good or evil. God wants us to choose good, of course, but allows the existence of the alternative because in the long run God's love is revealed in forgiveness.

We find that some of the most precious aspects of life are experienced because we have at times made evil choices. The experience of forgiveness and reconciliation can only follow real hurts. Humility follows the hard knocks and mistakes of life. Renewal often comes only after one hits "rock bottom." Compassion is evoked when people suffer hardships. Our ability to truly relate to the need of others is the product of our own, similar kind of need. It's not a perfect world by human standards. But through it all, God is with us, inviting us to respond to the imperfections in ways that redeem them by showing forth a greater glory, the glory of forgiveness, reconciliation, and renewal.

I would like to know if there is a good primer on the Christian faith. Is there one book you would recommend?

The source book on the Christian faith is actually a collection of books, the Hebrew and Greek Testaments of the Bible. I suggest you start with the prologue to the Gospel of John, the first 18 verses. Here, Christian faith is stated concisely and poetically. It's the best primer I know of. Then read the rest of the Gospel, which fills out the details of Jesus' life from a faith perspective.

The other Gospels, Matthew, Mark, and Luke, are called the Synoptic Gospels because they trace the life of Jesus more or less alike, although each view the biography of Jesus from different historical situations and contain particular emphases. Next, get to know St. Paul through his letters to the early Christians.

But, of course, you already know about the Bible. Beyond that, I would encourage you first to find a faith community in which to worship and study. When you find a church which resonates with you, you will be led to the catechism, or primer, of that community. Any book on Christian faith (including the Bible) is an interpretation of the faith. Even history written with academic discipline reflects the scholar's bias to some degree. And Christian faith cannot be captured purely in an historical account.

Seeking a primer on Christian faith is like seeking a primer on romantic love. Poets may come close to capturing its nuances and power, yet the reader enters the experience only vicariously. It cannot be reduced to statutes and categories. We do not rule the experience; it rules us. To truly learn of faith, one must give in to it.

To give in to Christian faith is to give in to Christian community. It has often been said that faith is not taught; it is caught. In the process of receiving the love of the extended family in the Body of Christ and sharing healing and growth experiences together, one catches the unconditional love of God. Christian communities are not perfect laboratories in which to learn moral codes, but they do provide plenty of practice in the art of forgiveness and reconciliation.

Faith is not contained in words, but power. You do not have to know all about faith in order to experience it. You do not have to wait until you are sure you have figured out the right religion before you practice faith. The mystery of God unfolds as we progress through life's portals and our humanity experiences the wonders of each stage in life's journey. Through it all, God is with us, and the love of God known in Jesus Christ gives us the ability to trust and respond with grace and courage. God's forgiveness picks us up when we fail and strengthens us through weakness. It's all about learning how to love as God loves us.

Faith cannot be found in a book. It is about community with God and neighbor. The Bible itself was not inspired apart from historical circumstances and needs of the faith communities of the Jewish and Christian people. St. Paul, by his own account, seems to have received one of the most dramatic of personal conversions, yet he refers to that part of his faith only briefly. The Christian scriptures attributed to Paul which inform our faith, however, are the by-product of pastoral concerns addressed by Paul to the churches he founded and sought to guide. They are, in a sense, inspired by the community experience of Christ, the dynamic between a people struggling to be faithful and an elder offering leadership.

The community gathered in worship - with each person bringing hurts, prayers and talents to be offered and blessed - is an inspiring celebration of God's rich creation, abiding presence and empowered purpose. During the liturgy one is invited to be set free from the prison of ego fulfillment and control and simply be washed in the ancient prayers and forms given contemporary expression by the gathered community of faith.

Faith is not a second-hand experience. Nor is it inherited or derived from membership in an organization. It is not captured in a book. Rather, it is a personal connection with God and one another in community.

I've always wondered what "fear of the Lord" means. I believe that God is love. Why does the Bible speak of fear?

Your question is a very important one. In Proverbs and the Psalms, there is the phrase, "Fear of the Lord is the beginning of wisdom." To be wise is to "fear" in the sense that scripture intends.

Awe and reverence is the usual interpretation of the biblical use of "fear." It is not being afraid of, but valuing God more than anything else. Think, for a moment, about what you value highly, say a loved one. Your greatest fear could be that you might lose that person. Fear of the Lord can be seen as fear that you might lose the Lord, or that the Lord might lose you!

Without God, our lives are ultimately meaningless and hopeless; whatever value there is in life is transient. With God, however, our lives have a purpose and a destination. With God, we are able to escape the prison of human narcissism and step into the freedom of life-giving mystery. With God, humanity can transcend the chronological moments of finite realities and enter the eternal, invisible truth and love which God expresses in creation. It is wise to treasure the mystery of God; it is foolish to give our passion to that which is passing away.

To elaborate a bit further, fear of the Lord contains certain ingredients. One is a sense of crisis, or urgency. It is the experience of being desperate, as in a foxhole conversion. There are times when any of us can be a believer because we will do anything to save ourselves. It is not that we fear the Lord, but we fear the situation and desperately ask the Lord to save us. If you take such a moment, which almost everyone experiences at least once in life, and project it over the whole of our lives, then you may get a sense of the desperate quality of life without God. While time and luxuries may delude us, the reality is that we are dead without God.

But fear of the Lord goes far beyond the foxhole conversion frame of mind. It is one thing to fear losing one's biological life. Once we allow ourselves to enter the sublime mysteries of God's presence, we discover a reality more wonderful than words can express. To cling to this grace and power and allow it to transform us is an important sense of fear of the Lord. If someone gave you a million dollars with no strings attached, you would not hesitate to take it, and yet many walk away from the invitation of God to receive the whole Kingdom!

There is still another important ingredient in fear of the Lord. It is called repentance. While we know there are no conditions on God's gifts to us, we do need to get out of the way to appreciate them fully. The basic human sin is that we want to be in charge. The reality is, however, that we are not in charge, and until we make peace with that, the Kingdom of God remains largely unavailable to us. We remain out in the cold by our own doing until we are ready to get on our knees (and I mean this literally if physically possible) and confess how we have foolishly tried to run our own lives, and dishonored God, our neighbors and ourselves. The next step is to correct the situation by inviting God to rule our lives and committing ourselves to do our best to let God rule us from here on out.

Christian faith is accepting Christ as Savior and promising to follow him as Lord. It means loving our neighbor as ourselves.

It also means working in the world for justice and peace and the dignity of all human beings and creation itself. Other faiths have their own ways of placing God first in their lives, and for Christians to say that our way is the only way regresses to our need to be in charge.

Fear of the Lord is not simply making God most important in our lives, but recognizing that God gives importance to all else. Without God we might as well not be. With God, to be is to become.

There's a part of the Lord's Prayer which confuses me. Jesus said to pray, "Lead us not into temptation." But why would God the Father lead us into temptation?

Y ou are not alone in your question. Christians have struggled with this phrase in the Lord's Prayer for centuries. At issue are some of the basic theological questions of the Christian experience of God.

First, we need to recognize that the Bible is translated into English from the original words which Jesus spoke, almost certainly in a semitic dialect called Aramaic. His words were recorded in the Gospels in the common Greek language of the day. The English you quote is from the "Authorized Version" of the Bible written in England in the early 17th Century under King James I.

Some linguistic scholars tell us that these words might better be understood as "Protect us from temptation" or even, "Help us to resist temptation." These translations, if accurate, give us a sense of God consistent with loving protection rather than implying that God would lead us into something that is harmful. I'm not a linguist, but I've learned to be suspicious of scholars' viewpoints which make the words of Jesus more acceptable to our preferred image of him.

Suppose we accept the words at face value as they appear in the familiar King James version. Why would God lead us into temptation? And, if God would, why would we pray for God not to?

We begin to sort this out by referring to the Gospel account of Jesus' own experience of temptation in the wilderness. The Synoptic Gospels (Matthew, Mark, and Luke) all record that Jesus was

71

sent by the spirit into the wilderness to be tempted by Satan. God must have had a reason. It is generally considered that Jesus' time in the wilderness facing up to the devil was both his final preparation for ministry and the demonstration of his once-and-for-all victory over evil to be won on the cross.

I believe Jesus taught us to pray "Lead us not into temptation" because he did for us what we cannot do for ourselves. By saying these words, we place our trust in the only one who can save us from evil, i.e., God, in the humanity of Jesus. To say this prayer does not mean that we want to be protected from temptation ourselves (although we can pray that prayer quite honestly). It means that we face temptation with the knowledge that Jesus has already won the victory for us.

Succumbing to temptation, therefore, has a different consequence for us as a result of Jesus. Evil no longer has the power to destroy us. Rather, God has the power to temper us through facing evil in the context of Grace.

If I were to put into my own words what Jesus meant, not based upon linguistic science, but upon my personal relationship with Jesus, I would say it this way: "Use our times of temptation to help us mature into the fullness of Christ."

God knows it has been those very times when I have succumbed to temptation which turned out in the long run to be what brought me to my knees.

> *Your "feel good" version of Christianity leads people away from true faith. God's law is clear in the Bible, and when you teach that violating the law is O.K. as long as you're "loving," as you did in your column on homosexuality, you help to undermine society's knowledge of right and wrong. People in your position should be strengthening our moral fiber, not undermining it.*

You and I probably have the same agenda, to help others grow closer to God and to live in ways that are right with God and people. One way to do this, as you suggest, is to see the Bible as a rule book, with laws laid out clearly to teach people right from

72

wrong. It provides order and a sense of security. This way is attractive because it seems that all we have to do is teach it and follow it.

However, people of faith might consider why Jesus confronted the religious leaders of his culture who practiced strict obedience to God's law. There were some essential flaws in their way of thinking.

First, obedience to the law seemed to pertain only to their external actions. While they satisfied the law technically, they violated the spirit of the law by setting themselves apart from others. Jesus confronted their feelings of superiority over others by noting that they, too, were guilty of violating the law in their hearts. In the familiar Sermon on the Mount, Jesus likened anger to killing and lust to adultery. Outward satisfaction is not enough. What is in the heart matters, too.

Second, the religious leaders were not fully obedient to the law anyway. In the story of the self-righteous stone throwers in the eighth chapter of John's Gospel (which tradition refers to as the story of the adulterous woman), Jesus reminds us that none of us can claim perfect obedience. Anyone who claims to satisfy the law is either a fool or a hypocrite.

Third, God's favor does not depend upon obedience to the law. The fact that Jesus "favored" sinners with his presence and affirmation was an affront to the whole basis of the conventional theology of the day, that one becomes right with God through obedience to God's laws. Jesus demonstrated in his life that we are right with God because God loves us. We do not have to obey to be loved. That is the Good News, and it invites us to live up to the status which God had given to humanity as heirs of the Kingdom. The Christian scriptures, particularly the writings of St. Paul, see the law as having served as custodian until the Spirit came to lead us.

Although Christians can be very legalistic, Christianity is essentially a faith which seeks to follow the Spirit of God as revealed in Jesus Christ, rather than the law. The Spirit does not replace the law, but fulfills it by leading us to do what is truly good and helpful for one's self and others. The law is consummated in our love for God and for neighbor as self. Such love is seen by Christians as the fulfillment of Jeremiah's prophecy in 31:33, "I will put my law within them, and will write it upon their hearts."

It is not an insult to me to suggest that mine is a "feel good" version of Christianity. The word Gospel literally means, "Good News." To "feel good" does not mean, however, that one can do whatever one wants.

Loving commitment toward friend, stranger, and enemy alike requires more of us than mere outward obedience to laws. Christian love involves an investment of one's heart as well as hands. It means viewing all people as important as family. It means giving up our need to control others, and to help them grow into the fullness of Christ's love for them and live responsible and loving lives. It means overcoming our fear and prejudice to build a caring community in which all people partake of God's blessings.

Traditionally, faith is presented by making people feel bad, then offering the chalice of forgiveness. But Jesus' way was to witness to the love of God by helping people to feel good about themselves. Then he invited them to follow him.

The New Testament is blatantly anti-Semitic. How do you explain the long history of Christian prejudice against Jews, beginning with your own scriptures?

I agree that there are anti-Semitic elements in the new Testament (which I prefer to call the Christian scriptures). This is not surprising, considering the great divorce which gradually unfolded between the Judaism of biblical times and emerging Christianity, which began as a Jewish sect.

Christians tell the history of Jesus in the four Gospels: Matthew, Mark, Luke and John. By today's standards, these would not be considered completely accurate historical accounts, but are often referred to as "Spiritual history." This means that the storytellers related not only the event as they experienced it or heard of it, but also incorporated in the story their own faith perspective.

Even secular historians of biblical times wrote such interpretive history, often from the bias of whoever was ruler when the history was written. With regard to Jesus, this ancient custom has spawned a great search for the historical Jesus among scholars who seek to ferret out the true history from the spin of storytellers.

Few scholars today would question the general outline of the Gospel story. Jesus was a remarkable Jewish teacher who confronted the established leadership of his religious community, the Scribes, Pharisees and Saducees. These parties of Jewish authority were represented in the Sanhedrin, the court of law for Judaism. Jesus was brought before the presiding high priest, who, while finding no evidence to convict Jesus of charges of heresy, nonetheless referred him to the Roman court at the suggestion that he was stirring up a revolution against Caesar.

The Roman governor, likewise, found no evidence upon which to convict Jesus. The crowds, however, stirred up by the Jews who were determined to eliminate Jesus, demanded his death. Pilate, with more passion for tranquillity than truth, granted their wishes. After Jesus' death, his followers began to report his return as Risen Lord.

While Jesus lived in the context of Judaism, the story is not about any particular race, but about all of humanity. It is about the misuse of religious and secular power common to all times and places. The story of Jesus confronts all of us in our need to maintain established human traditions in the face of God's call to the future.

It is the story of God's breaking open our secure order of social hierarchy. It is the story of the desire we all have to make God into our own image, and the anger we experience when our expectations of God are not met.

The Gospels and the letters of Christian scripture are reflective of the hostility which soon arose between Jews and Christians. The Gospels' message of salvation and transformation lies not in the specifics of the people involved, but in the universal traits those people share with all of us.

The great failure of Christianity over the centuries is that we have not identified with the biblical religious establishment, the Jews of the Gospels. We have not allowed Jesus to confront us as people of faith. Rather, we have let our traditions around Jesus set us apart from the rest of humanity as we stand in righteous judgment over them. Judgment of others has no place in Christian faith.

The long history of prejudice from Christians toward Jews (and others) represents a tragic failure of Christian leaders to practice, if not to hear, the liberating power of the Gospel. We have no one to blame but ourselves for the crucifixion of Jesus in our own day.

*You have referred to eternal
life experienced in this world, but did not explain what
this means. What is the difference between eternal life
as a present reality and eternal life as a future reality?*

In its literal sense, eternal life is life which has no ending. This, of course, is not part of reality in this world. No one has yet found the legendary fountain of youth!

The word "eternal" in the biblical sense, however, is much richer. Its chronological aspect is only one of many aspects which imbue it with meaning. Christian scriptures reveal that eternal life begins not after we die, but when we know God revealed in Jesus Christ. Jesus is quoted to say in John 17:3 as he prays to the Father, "And this is eternal life, that they may know you, the only true God and Jesus Christ whom you have sent."

Eternal life is, therefore, not merely a quantitative experience, but a qualitative one. When we know God in the way that God comes to us in Jesus we find eternal life. It becomes a synonym for fellowship with God.

Christian theology speaks of eternal life in this world because God has come to humanity in the person of Jesus Christ. Because of the Incarnation, we can experience heaven on earth, even though we are still subject to the limitations of our humanity. We are in the world, yet not of the world.

Many Christian readers, however, will take issue with me when I suggest that our faith teaches us not to think that we are the only ones who know God as Jesus reveals God. Eternal life is experienced in the world by many who lack a personal relationship with Jesus Christ. This is because they have the Spirit of Christ written upon their hearts and they bear the fruit of the Spirit in their lives.

Paul says in Romans 2:14-16, "When Gentiles, who do not

possess the law, do instinctively what the law requires, these, though not having the law, are a law to themselves. They show that what the law requires is written on their hearts, to which their own conscience also bears witness; and their conflicting thoughts will accuse or perhaps excuse them on the day when, according to my gospel, God, through Jesus Christ, will judge the secret thoughts of all." His reasoning with regard to Gentiles and the Jewish law might also be applied to non-Christians with regard to the love of Christ.

And in Galatians 5:22 we are told of the fruits of the Spirit, "...the fruit of the Spirit is love, joy, peace, patience, kindness, generosity, faithfulness, gentleness, and self control." Where the fruit is, there is the Spirit.

Eternal life is a gift from God. The ingredients of such life have always been present because Christ and the Holy Spirit are always present where God is present. Christians articulate how this is possible through the Doctrine of the Holy Trinity, but this only describes our experience of God, while God initiates it. The Doctrine of the Trinity does not limit the experience of God to Christians.

The prophet Micah states the qualities of eternal life succinctly: "He has told you, O Mortal, what is good; and what does the Lord require of you but to do justice, and to love kindness, and to walk humbly with your God?" Any life which is lived thankfully as a child of God in response to the gracious love of God, and seeks to express itself through love for neighbors, can be said to be an eternal life because it is life as God intends it to be lived.

> *It is very hard for me to accept that human beings are born sinful, which is what I understand the Doctrine of Original Sin to mean, essentially. I believe we learn how to sin. Please express your thoughts on original sin.*

We often think of sin as an act or thought which is against the will of God. Human beings are born with a sense of self which many people throughout time have struggled to define. The self includes a will to have things our way, which can be very problematic with regard to relationships, beginning with our relationship with God.

Adam and Eve ate from the Tree of the Knowledge of Good and Evil because they wanted to decide for themselves what was good and what was evil. In doing so they were not doing a dastardly deed: they were doing what was natural for them as human beings - expressing their self-will. They entered the lonely and frightening human dilemma of being in charge of their lives while not having the tools to make life work. The story of the Fall, as it is called, contains the elements of what is common to all humanity in relationship to God and neighbor; we are separated by the sense of self and the willfulness which naturally follows.

It is important for us to become in touch with the original sin which we all carry. We have a self-will and we are unable to exercise it fully. Restraints are placed upon us from the moment we leave our mother's womb and begin to realize that we are, biologically at least, on our own. Gradually we learn to accept our limitations, but there is a degree of frustration and anger engendered in the process.

To deal with original sin, we must learn to deal, therefore, with our anger. Another way to say this is that we must learn to forgive. Jesus said he came to proclaim the forgiveness of God, and we generally accept this as God's forgiveness of us for our self-will, or for original sin. But have you ever considered that part of the message of forgiveness is our need to forgive God?

The fact is that the world is not created the way we would like it to be. I've already noted how we would like to be in charge, but of course we are not. A few of us by skill and resources may gain great worldly power, and many of us find enough to lead relatively peaceful lives. Some resort to violence because it is the only way they can sense a degree of power in their lives. But underlying each of our lives is a subtle anger with God - jealously, really - because we are not God.

So you and I have a problem. While we may take some comfort in the fact that each human being who has ever lived has had the same problem, it looms in the core of our soul as though we were the only person whom God ever created.

Of course, God provides a way out of this dilemma: It's called

Grace. God invites us to give our lives as a gift back to our creator and to follow the path intended for us from the beginning, revealed through God's teaching in history found definitively in God's own incarnation in Jesus Christ. It is in this sense that God saves us from sin and from the consequences of the dilemma described above. But to give our lives to God we first have to get over being mad. Once we truly acknowledge that the self stands in the way of true intimacy with God, then we are on the way to healing and renewal. Then we might do well to get in touch with the chronic anger upon which we have built our lives and realize the degree to which we have built them upon sand. We might look at certain hurts and failures through the lens of our anger with God and see how we have lashed out at others (or ourselves) inappropriately and un-knowingly.

Original sin came with original forgiveness, and the sooner we hook the two back together again , the better our lives - and the world - will be.

> *I once heard an evangelist list all of the places in the Old Testament where the love of Christ was present. He said, for example, that Jesus Christ was the rock from which water poured for the people in the desert. My question is this, "Why is the 'New Testament' new? Isn't the love of God unchang-ing?"*

Your question focuses upon an important issue for Christian the-ology and Jewish/Christian relationships. The traditional teaching of the word "new," as in "New Testament," is that the "Christ event" in all of its aspects initiated a new covenant of grace which replaced the old covenant of law. Prior to this action of God in history, humanity was enslaved by the dilemma that obedience brings righteousness, yet obedience is impossible. We simply could not become right with God through our own efforts.

In Christ, God acted to make us right. Our status with God became no longer a matter of our obedience to the law, but rather a matter of trusting in the law of God received unconditionally through Jesus Christ. In other words, through faith.

Of course, it was not God who changed, but rather our perception of God. Because of Jesus the understanding of God's nature was so dramatically different that early Christians used such expressions as "new creation" and "The old has passed away and the new has begun." One could list many examples, but suffice it to say from the experience of those who came to know Jesus as risen Lord, reality was indeed new.

But Christian faith is more than the existential awareness of truth about God's nature. It is also that this awareness is possible only because of what God has done in Jesus Christ. In the deeper cosmic sense, God changed the possibilities for humanity and for creation, which is to say, God made creation new. It is in the "Word made flesh" where what it is to be human is changed forever.

God redeemed the past and made our future secure by entering our humanity. This new action was not the replacement of the old, but rather its fulfillment. It has lead us to replace some of the ways we thought and acted toward God (and one another), but it was not a replacement of God's disposition toward us, which has always been forgiving and loving. This continuity between the "old" and "new" is what is meant by your question.

I'm trying to get into the habit of referring to Old and New Testaments as the Hebrew and the Greek scriptures in order to lose the subtle inference that one replaces the other and that Christians and Jews worship a different God. The Christ event was indeed new, but it was the manifestation of the eternal heart of God. Christians have a lot to learn from Jews, just as the Greek scriptures are meaningful in the context of the Hebrew scriptures.

For Christians to feel superior to Jews (or anyone) because they have something new is to miss the point of what it is to be Christian. We easily forget Jesus' words, "Whoever would be great among you must be your servant and whoever would be first among you must be slave of all."

BIBLICAL INSPIRATION

I've been told that some people who claim to be Christians don't really believe in the Bible. Have you heard this, and what is your perspective with regard to the Bible?

I'm glad you asked this question because it raises one of the most divisive issues in the church today. It is commonplace to see accusations from both conservatives and liberals that those who disagree with them are untrue to the faith. Conservatives generally say that liberals are not Bible-believing, and liberals say that conservatives don't understand the Bible, or are unwilling to.

The Bible is unique in literature as the revelation of God through history, beginning with creation, then the covenant with the Hebrew people and, finally, with all of humanity through Jesus Christ. All Christians believe the Bible to be central to the faith. All, as far as I know, believe the Bible to be the inspired word of God.

When one says someone else does not believe in the Bible, it usually means that person doesn't interpret the Bible literally. There is a pervasive myth among Christians that there is one literal truth revealed in scripture. Added to this is the idea that anyone who does not see the one truth is unbelieving. But, of course, even among those who profess this there is great diversity in interpretation and application.

The fact is that scripture reveals God's love for humankind as an evolving, dynamic, complex series of events loosely based on history, with theologians filling in the gaps and embellishing the events to reveal their meaning. This imprecise, yet formative story is the common ground of faith. (The Hebrew for Jews, and the Hebrew and Greek portions for Christians.)

It is the word of God because the church at one point in history declared it to contain all that is necessary for salvation. The golden thread of God's truth and love is woven through the variety of forms of literature in scripture as authors seek to interpret human life in the light of God's revelation.

I suppose I would be labeled as a liberal with regard to the Bible. This means that I can allow for a particular passage to be worthy of more than one interpretation. It means that I struggle with the meaning of the passage as it was intended when it was written and how that meaning applies today. It means that I accept the widely held view among Christians that the stories evolved in oral tradition long before they were written and that they were embellished and refined to better make the point of the storyteller.

A liberal view understands that any given book of the Bible may have more than one author, although only one is cited. Editing may have taken several generations. It means that not all parts of the scripture were intended to be taken literally, and I have to struggle with what is intended to be literal and what isn't.

These are just some of the aspects of the so-called liberal point of view. Actually, the liberal perspective is based upon a very conservative theology, i.e., the Holy Spirit leads the one who meditates upon the word of God (as well as the rest of life) into all truth, as Jesus promised.

You see, faith is not static activity which lives in the dead words of the past, but a dynamic, responsive relationship with God in the present. God inspired scripture and inspires the reader today when scripture is used prayerfully with both mind and heart. When we try to narrow the meaning of scripture to a legalistic interpretation of words on a page, we turn our backs on the Lord, who seeks to ignite our hearts with passion in the here and now.

The fear, of course, is that once interpretation is allowed, then anything goes. The safeguard against this is love. God's love, revealed in scripture, is intended to heal and transform immoral and destructive attitudes and behavior into life-giving relationships. And without such love, even a literal truth can be abused, as St. Paul so eloquently states in 1 Corinthians 13.

We live in fearful times, when there is a tendency to cling to certainty and look outside of ourselves for simplistic answers. Tthere is also a tendency to find solace in the idea that we are right and others are wrong. Our Judeo-Christian tradition shows us a better, wiser way. Why place our ultimate trust in scripture as law when the scriptures themselves invite us into a personal, loving and community-building fellowship with the lawgiver?

*Please interpret Jesus'
words, "Let the dead bury their dead."*

These words of Jesus make two essential points of Christian spirituality. First, they mark the radical claim which God's Lordship has upon our lives. Second, they suggest that the way of God demonstrated in Jesus' own life is in contrast to the way of the world.

The words are quoted in the gospels of Matthew and Luke. In both instances, Jesus has invited people to follow him, and one of those present says that he will follow after he returns home to bury his father.

While we may surmise that Jesus is not unsympathetic to the need for the man's presence with his family, he also knows that the decision to follow him is one which cannot be postponed. Following Jesus is a matter of deciding in the here and now whether one will be led by the Spirit of God or by the values of the world.

The man to whom Jesus spoke was caught in the historical circumstance of having to choose between one place or another. He could not be in two places at the same time, and so choosing to follow Jesus, to follow the way of life rather than the way of death, was Jesus' invitation to him. Today, we are able to follow Jesus as Risen Lord wherever we may be. We have the ability to submit our commitments to family and others to the larger context of the love of Christ.

The love of God, then, takes precedence over any other commitments we may have. While we can live out God's love in our daily lives with family and friends, when we are forced to choose, our loyalty to God's call to us comes first.

This brings us to the second point. Family ways are usually infected with the world's values, and when we begin to take Jesus seriously as our Lord, we find that we run into conflict within ourselves and our relationships.

Families are wonderful instruments of the love of God. They also tend to restrict such love to members of the family. The world says "Blood is thicker than water" as a way of separating family from others. Jesus says, in effect, "We are all of one blood." As powerful as family love is, it also teaches a we/they view of the world, where non-family persons are reduced to people of lesser status.

Loyalties may extend to a tribe or a community, or to a nation, but the line is drawn somewhere. The invisible lines of commitment may also be drawn where there are economic or educational differences, and certainly where there are behavioral differences.

In the midst of the great cry to return to family values, we must be alert to the dangers of thinking of family in a narrow sense. Family ties can be the source of great division and hostility, where people see one another as threats to their own security rather than as partners in the human endeavor.

One of the institutions which Jesus came to confront is the family. This is not to say that families cannot be nurturing places, but simply that they tend to be narrowly focused. The protective instincts which family engender cause human beings to seek the refuge of hierarchical power structures which establish and enforce controls to keep order.

This worldly way of being is called the "Myth of Redemptive Violence" by Walter Wink, a prominent Biblical scholar and theologian. In short, it says that life is made up of good guys and bad guys. It is the duty of the good guys to win over the bad guys, and the way to do it is through power, and if necessary, violence.

It lies at the core of the hierarchical model of the traditional family, our sense of patriotism as a nation, and has been the dominant force in church history. It is not the way of Jesus, however, who lived and taught servanthood rather than forceful dominance.

If you would like to explore further why Jesus might have said "Let the dead bury their dead" and some of the ideas I have stated above, I recommend that you read, The Chalice and the Blade, by Riane Eisler. It is an interesting portrayal of the contrast between the hierarchical, defensive model of our life together and the model of our humanity as partners made in the image of God.

BIBLICAL INSPIRATION

Your liberal ideas are offensive to God and to true Christians. I wonder if you even believe in the resurrection of Jesus, or if you are like one of your Episcopal bishops, John Spong, who thinks it is only a story made up by early Christians.

While I can't compare my views with your characterization of Bishop Spong's, I would be happy to describe for you my own understanding of the resurrection.

In his first letter to the Corinthians, Paul speaks extensively about Jesus' resurrection. Readers should refer to Chapter 15. Paul places Jesus' crucifixion and resurrection in the context of Hebrew hope for a messiah. He establishes the historical eyewitness accounts of the resurrection of Jesus by citing the order of appearances to his followers.

Finally, he witnesses to his own encounter with Jesus as Risen Lord. It is upon these personal encounters and the personal experience of Jesus through the centuries and in our own time that the resurrection is proven.

The resurrection is the cornerstone of Christian doctrine and practice because without it there is no basis for understanding Jesus in any other way than as a great person in history. Without the resurrection, there is no basis for understanding Jesus as God incarnate in the world.

As Paul continues to say in 1 Corinthians 15:13, "If there is no resurrection of the dead, then Christ has not been raised; and if Christ has not been raised, then our proclamation has been in vain and your faith has been in vain."

It is important to remind ourselves that essential matters of faith cannot be explained or proven scientifically. Arguing that the resurrection violates the laws of nature falls upon the deaf ears of those of us who experience reality beyond the physical. As Jesus said, "With God all things are possible." Faith is not based upon creation alone, but upon the creator.

Likewise, believers will never convince unbelievers who require physical proof. Put simply, the resurrection of the dead is a matter of faith, not science. Christian attempts to use scientific proof are seen as foolishness by unbelievers, and rightfully so.

The Doctrine of the Resurrection is this - that God made it possible for humanity to have an ongoing personal relationship with Jesus beyond the grave. How this is true we cannot explain, but it is true for those who trust enough to give their hearts to him. In Jesus, humanity encounters not simply a spokesman for God, but God.

Death was not the end of God's revelation in Christ. Rather, Jesus' undeserved and terrible death was the very means God chose to express personal and forgiving love for the world. The return of Jesus in forgiveness and his invitation to restore fellowship and follow him, is the guarantee that nothing can separate us from the love of God, not even our own sins.

Paul seems impatient with those who want to try to explain the resurrection in rational ways.

Do I believe in the resurrection of Jesus? You bet I do. To say less would be to say that I don't know Jesus personally as my Lord and Savior. I could not betray him in such a way because all that he has done in my life would be a lie. I struggle each day with my ability to follow him and to share his love with others, and while I sometimes don't hold up my side of the relationship very well, I never have doubted that Jesus is with me and holding up his.

Would you write one of your columns on the Book of Revelation? How does it relate to heaven and redemption?

No book of the bible is more misused or less understood than the Book of Revelation. In mainline churches it tends not to be taken too seriously. In some churches, it is, perhaps, given too much emphasis.

Some churches seem to have built their whole theology upon this last book of the Bible, giving it more importance than the Gospels themselves.

It is one of my favorite books of the Bible because of its basic message of trust, its wonderful imagery and symbolism and its focus upon Jesus as the savior of the world.

The message of Revelation might be summarized this way: "When you are feeling deserted by God and persecuted by the world,

86

try not to despair and, above all, don't stop trusting God. Your trial does not mean that the loving God we know in Christ is not in charge. God's love will prevail and be vindicated in due time. God's plan of salvation is unfolding, despite appearances.

Apocalyptic literature arose in pre-Christian Hebrew times out of the frustration of unfulfilled hopes for a worldly kingdom. Such literature suggests a heavenly kingdom, ushered in by the end of the created order as we know it and the beginning of a new creation, a heavenly Jerusalem. The Book of Daniel and parts of Ezekiel are the most popular of this genre of literature.

Revelation is the Christian expression of the appeal to remain loyal to God while under the persecution of false rulers. It consists of a series of visions revealed to St. John. It is not a literal prediction of the future. Its message is timeless. It is misused when interpreted as though the images were intended to be metaphors for actual historical events, people, or places of today. Such interpretations, while fascinating, may cause the reader to miss the underlying current of God's love.

It is sometimes used as a tool for conversion, in effect to frighten people into believing or to bribe them with promises of heaven. If we remember that it was written to impart courage to the faithful, not to convert unbelievers, then we are on the right track of discovering its value in Holy Scripture.

Many, including Martin Luther, have voiced an uneasiness with Revelation. It does seem less than Christian in some ways. The wrath of God so violently expressed seems inconsistent with the Jesus of the Gospels. Where is the message to love one's enemies? Where is the forgiveness of those who persecute you? Where is the call to the faithful to be humble servants of others?

Instead, Revelation gives comfort by promising revenge. While this appeals to our nature, it is not the shining glory of God's love which pours from the lips and hands of Jesus. These faults, however, are characteristic of apocalyptic literature and must be seen as the package of the revelation, not the revelation itself. Remember, Revelation begins and ends with Jesus Christ. When it appears at times to be contrary to Jesus, the writer would want us, I think, to go with Jesus.

In a world so prone to violence and persecution, we do not

need to use any part of the Bible as a justification for diminishing the value of others. We can know that God is on our side without needing to know that God is against others. Such a perspective helps us all to be more aware of our own faults and more open to the goodness of our fellow human beings - even those who persecute us.

*A friend who is a seminary
graduate tells me that the Book of Revelation is really
nothing more than an "encoded" language meant only
for those of long ago through which they were warned
of horrors to come to them at the hands of their Roman
tormentors, and never meant to have any meaning for
us. I'd like to hear your response to this.*

The Book of Revelation is part of a genre of biblical literature called "apocalyptic." Revelation is the Latin for the Greek word, "Apocalypse." It did indeed grow out of Hebrew literature which began to see the fulfillment of God's promises, not in the establishment of a political and geographical kingdom, but in the creation of a new, transcendent order of creation brought into being by the intervention of God.

Apocalyptic literature has several characteristics. Holding no hope for the present order alleged to be dominated by evil forces, it anticipates the imminent action of God to establish a new order. It views present reality as inevitably horrible, yet short lived. The encoded language to which you refer is typical of such literature, and speaks of evil authorities in discreet ways in order to gain wide circulation without incurring suppression from political authorities.

It is true that the message was intended for certain people in an historical setting. The essence of the message, however, is applicable in all times and places, particularly for someone who is experiencing great hardship.

The message of apocalyptic literature is this: Don't let the painful circumstances you are enduring weaken your faith. It may not seem so, but God is in charge, and God loves you.

This time of suffering is short compared to the joy waiting for those who trust in God.

Christian apocalyptic literature, such as Revelation, places Jesus Christ as the instrument of God's salvation. God has defeated the forces of evil through the Christ event in history.

Through fantastic imagery, the Book of Revelation proclaims the reality of evil in the world, but more importantly the ultimate defeat of evil already accomplished. It tells of the birth of Jesus, his ministry, his death and resurrection, and even the worship and ministry of the church - all in encoded language. It also vividly describes those who persecute the church.

Revelation is intended, therefore, to give those who suffer (and we all have such times to some degree) a larger perspective. We should not be surprised, but prepared. It is not part of God's plan to remove suffering from our lives.

It is a misuse of Revelation to try to decode the symbolism as if it refers to current events. It refers to the events of the time in which it was written. Its relevance today is not that it predicted the details of history, but that it strengthens our faith as we face the same issues and trials that were faced then.

We hope that we never have to suffer, let alone to suffer persecution. Yet, we cannot deny that it is a part of life. While we work to create a more loving world, it is important to trust that when it is unloving, God will strengthen our faith and use us to encourage others.

By the way, the Book of Revelation should never be referred to as "Revelations." Always use the singular. It's a dead giveaway that someone quoting it really doesn't know much about it.

How would you address Revelation 22:7 and also 22:18-19?

For the benefit of readers, these passages are as follows: "'Listen!' says Jesus. 'I am coming soon! Happy are those who obey the prophetic words in this book!'....I, John, solemnly warn everyone who hears the prophetic words of this book: If anyone adds anything to them, God will add to his punishment the plagues described in this book. And if anyone takes anything away from the prophetic words of this book, God will take away from him his share of the fruit of the tree of life and of the Holy City, which are described in this book."

These words are part of the concluding verses of the Revelation of John, the last book in the Christian Bible. They are characteristic of apocalyptic literature because they contain a sense of urgency, a dire warning, the use of symbolic imagery, and an imminent, cataclysmic focus.

Apocalyptic literature arose from the hopelessness of times of persecution and the consequent confusion of the faithful in a world where evil seems to have the upper hand. Apocalyptic seeks to strengthen the faithful, discourage apostasy, and provide assurance that God's justice will come to light.

Specifically, the Book of Revelation is attributed to John in his elderly years while exiled on the island of Patmos. He records for the early church, suffering enormously under the persecution of Nero, the Roman emperor, a series of visions and messages he received from the Risen Christ. Surely Revelation was afforded the distinction of being the final book of the Bible because of these expectant words before the blessing, "Come, Lord Jesus."

One must understand the verses you quoted in the context of their historical setting and the nature of apocalyptic literature. Essentially, it says this: "Don't let the present circumstances confuse you. The love of God which we know in Jesus Christ is in charge. Pay no allegiance to any other god (adding to these words) nor doubt the verity of what has been revealed to you (taking away from them), because without trust in Jesus' words you cannot experience eternal life (using the punitive language that God will punish or withhold fruit).

Through John, Jesus Christ assures humanity that he has already delivered the mortal blow to evil, although evil still has some limited earthly power, and that he will return soon to eliminate evil altogether. What the resulting "new creation" will look like exactly is not clear, but there will be no evil, and as these verses suggest, humanity will be restored to oneness with God and fullness of life.

The irony of Revelation and all of apocalyptic literature is that what it foretells has already happened. Evil and death were defeated by God in Jesus Christ's death and resurrection. Revelation is not intended, therefore, to serve a future purpose, but a present one, and it is based upon the actions of God in the past. From the Christian perspective, times of persecution are opportunities to deepen one's faith, to demonstrate trust in God when it is costly to do so, and to proclaim God's ways amid worldly values.

Revelation has always been a controversial part of Christian literature because it stresses retribution rather than the forgiveness of Christ, and because it implies that right behavior rather than trust gains salvation. And its hostility toward enemies certainly stands in contrast to Jesus' teaching in the Gospels. These weaknesses are more than controverted by the larger context of the Gospel message, however, which is why Revelation should always be understood in that light.

Don't take the verses above as an excuse to exclude anyone from the Gospel's embrace. Rather, take them as an assurance that nothing more and nothing less is needed, save God's love for us.

I am 10 years old, and I asked my Sunday School teacher a question which she said I should ask you. "If God is neither male nor female, how did Mary get pregnant?"

That's a very good question. I hereby dub you a first-class theologian! Anyone who asks questions about God is a theologian. Your Sunday School teacher should be commended for creating an environment in your classroom where questions can be asked.

The best answer to your question is to say that anything is possible for God. After all, didn't God create both the egg and the sperm in the first place? In every birth, God acts through the mother and father because God created mothers and fathers.

God wanted to become human and asked for Mary's cooperation as Jesus' mother. Jesus would be the surest sign of God's desire to be with humanity. He would also be a model for human beings to follow. And, in Jesus, God could do for humanity what we could not otherwise do, to provide whatever is needed to be with God. God came to be with us so that we could be with God forever.

The stories of Jesus' birth express the experience of God in Jesus, and were written after the resurrection of Jesus, when the disciples realized that Jesus was still with them, even though he had been crucified and died.

You need to be aware of the fact that there is some controversy around your question. Some Christians think Jesus' birth literally happened as the Bible says and others think it may not have. Don't be troubled by this. The basic truth is the same: Jesus is God as a human being. God loves us so much that Jesus came to invite us to be with him forever. Everyone is invited - no exceptions! All we have to do is accept the invitation!

Now I want to tell you a story. When my son was about your age, a friend of his came and knocked on our door, asking if he could play. Unfortunately, John was ill, so I went to the door to tell John's friend that John could not come out to play. His friend greeted me with enthusiasm and a big smile, but when he found out that John couldn't play, his face dropped. He went away sad, but not before asking me to tell John that he hoped he felt better soon.

I wondered later whether John's friend was sad because John was sick or because he wouldn't have John to play with. Was he sorry for John or for himself? I realized it was probably both. He was disappointed not to have a playmate, and he felt sorry for John, too.

Jesus is God knocking on our door wanting to play. He knocks, but for one reason or another we don't always come out to play. Maybe we have a kind of sickness which prevents us from being with him. It might be that we're afraid, or we let our doubts get in the way, or we think that if we play with Jesus, we are choosing one religion over another. Many times Jesus goes away sad, yet he always comes back to knock again, just checking to see, not if we're able, but if we're willing, to play.

Derek, as you grow up, a lot of questions will arise in your mind about your faith. This is very healthy, and I hope you will struggle with them seriously. That's the way you get to know God yourself instead of simply accepting what others tell you. One of the greatest gifts you can give to God is to use the mind God gave you to question your ideas in the light of new experiences and knowledge. But there is one thing you can trust in and don't need to question: God is with you and loves you.

*Catholics believe that Mary,
the mother of our Lord, remained a virgin after Jesus
was born and never had other children. Didn't she and
Joseph have children?*

It was not until the fourth century after Christ that the great
scholar and linguist St. Jerome argued successfully for the wide-
spread idea that Mary remained a virgin after giving birth to Jesus.
The biblical evidence is that Jesus had up to four brothers, James,
Joseph, Simon and Jude. They are mentioned quite simply as brothers of the Lord. By the time of Jerome, however, the gradual eleva-
tion of Mary in the devotional life of the Church led to the interpretation that these early church figures were actually cousins of the
Lord, sons of another Mary, the wife of Cleopas.

Protestants tend to place priority upon the straightforward
biblical evidence, and therefore accept that Jesus had brothers.
Roman Catholics stress church teaching to interpret scripture and
therefore generally accept the view that Mary remained a virgin.

I leave it to you to decide for yourself by referring to the pertinent passages, Mark 6:3, John 7:3, Acts 1:14, and 1 Corinthians
9:5. You will also find it helpful to speak with a priest or minister
about your church's teaching on the matter.

Your question raises the issue of authority. Does one accept
the biblical evidence alone, or does one accept the teaching of the
church even when it seems to contradict the natural sense of the
Bible or go beyond what the Bible says? And, is there room for
personal interpretation?

We are wise to allow the Bible the spiritual authority which
is claimed for it by the church. The Bible is our "canon." This
means that leaders of the church have certified it to contain all
that is necessary for salvation.

The historical Jesus is understood by Christians to be the
definitive interpretation not only of the rest of the Bible, but of all
of life, because Jesus is God coming into our midst as a human.

Many Protestant churches leave it there. "The Bible says
what it says and that is that." Of course, it is not that simple. The
Bible is capable of varied interpretations. Anyone who says that it
is not simply chooses to be blind to other viewpoints. The Bible

itself is a witness to the evolving interpretation of historical events and the experience of God.

For example, the Jesus experienced by the author of Mark's Gospel is quite different from the Jesus known by John and the community behind John's Gospel. We see Jesus through the eyes of his beholders, which means that he is interpreted through the worship and story traditions of those who knew him in the flesh and those who knew him only as Risen Lord.

It wasn't until three centuries after Jesus that the Bible became canonized, and the time had long since passed when we could have discerned the historical Jesus from the Jesus of faith. The Gospels portray a mixture of both, and much modern scholarship speculates upon knowing one from the other.

So, the Bible itself is the product of tradition. Revelation is no less inspired by God because it is interpreted by the life situations of the writers.

One must weigh both the Bible and subsequent church teaching while deciding what truth is. This is the role of the individual believer, using the faculties of reason and intuition in the context of a sincere and humble desire to know God. We must try to make our decisions in the light of the multiple authorities of scripture, tradition, and the Holy Spirit within us.

Did Jesus have brothers and perhaps even sisters? You know what the Bible says and what the Roman Catholic tradition says. What is your best sense of it as you apply reason and intuition, listening to the Holy Spirit within you?

Someone I trust recently told me that the biblical stories of Jesus' birth are legendary. Is that true?

No one knows exactly the historical accuracy of the Gospel stories.

They are based on historical events in the life of Jesus Christ, but they are also influenced by the faith of those who recount them. The Gospel writers were inspired by their knowledge of the oral and written tradition of the early Church, the Hebrew scriptures, and the pastoral concerns of their own historical setting.

The fact that these influences would color the limited knowledge they might have had of Jesus' birth should not surprise or threaten the faith of believers. The stories are no less inspired by God because of "legendary" elements.

It is best to understand the Gospels as "spiritual history." The inspired writers are intent on revealing not only the historical events, but even more importantly, the meaning of the events for those who believe in Jesus as Lord and Savior.

As for the Christmas story, only two Gospels record it, Matthew and Luke. Neither Mark nor John were concerned with the birth stories of Jesus.

Based upon the Gospels themselves, therefore, we must ask, why are these powerful stories not included in both Mark and John? There are several possibilities, but at least one of them is that they did not develop until later in the tradition of the early church. While we cannot be certain, there is much to support this argument.

Matthew was writing to Christians largely from Jewish backgrounds. He was careful, therefore, to appeal to the knowledge and sensitivities of people who saw in Jesus the fulfillment of their Messianic expectations and were struggling with their Jewish roots. We see this influence, perhaps, where Joseph, not Mary, is the one through whom God reveals the true meaning of the events surrounding Jesus' birth, and it is Joseph who receives God's guidance and responds faithfully.

In Luke, however, Mary is in the limelight. God works directly with her not only in the divine circumstances of her pregnancy, but also in its interpretation and subsequent action. This is probably because Luke's audience consists largely of Gentiles who have become Christians. He was almost certainly a Gentile himself. Luke is able to affirm women as worthy of God's revelation without their male covering, and in the response of Mary he underscores the significance of Jesus for all of humanity, with or without Hebrew tradition.

Both Matthew and Luke reflect the circumstances of second-generation Christianity. The birth stories were not important to the earliest followers, and by the time of Matthew and Luke, much may have been constructed.

Faith should not be based upon absolute historical accuracy

of the birth stories of Jesus. Historical accuracy is simply not possible, and if it were, the events still could not stand on their own as a basis for faith. It is not the events alone, but what they reveal which changes our lives. The Gospels record and interpret historical events and it is all part of God's inspiration.

If we hold to literal historical accuracy as a basis for faith, then we found our faith on facts subject to suspicion. But if we use the stories to inform and enliven our relationship with God then we enter into the experience of a loving God and continue the living history of the good news revealed in the Bible.

If the birth stories of Jesus cannot be believed as historical fact, how can anyone be expected to believe in the resurrection? You said in a recent column that much in the birth stories "may have been constructed." Constructed is a polite way of saying made up, which means a lie. If you don't believe in the historical accuracy of God's word, then that must include the resurrection of Jesus. Why believe in the resurrection stories and not the birth stories?

I've received a number of letters from people surprised that a priest would not accept the complete historical accuracy of the birth stories of Jesus as recorded in the Gospels of Luke and Matthew. If you took a poll of clergy who do not always interpret the Bible as literal history, I suspect most of them would agree that at least parts of the story were constructed based upon Hebrew scripture and the writer's desire to interpret the significance of Jesus' birth in the context of his own historical setting. This is what seminaries of all mainline and Roman Catholic denominations have been teaching for decades and does not imply a lack of faith in the Resurrection.

For Christians, the historical evidence of the resurrection of Jesus Christ lies not only in the biblical narrative, but in one's relationship with the risen Lord. The biblical accounts are the witness of such relationships, not intended to be science as we know it today. Biblical writers were evangelists, not modern scientists. While we are encouraged and taught by the witness of the Bible, the saints, and Christians today, it is our own encounter with Jesus which proves he lives as Risen Lord and Savior. The Resurrection is therefore the only necessary evidence and the only provable evidence of his identity.

Based on the reality of the Risen Jesus in early Christians' lives, it was important to tell and retell the stories of his historical life and ministry. At first, these stories were mostly about his final days and death on the cross. Gradually, the events of his life were recounted and assembled in an order logical and useful to the evangelists. Eventually the stories were recorded in four Gospels, each with its own perspective. Some stories, and even some Gospels, did not make it into the Bible as finally approved in the Fourth Century.

Little was known about Jesus' childhood, so little is recorded. Even the casual reader of the Bible might question why the birth of Jesus is recorded in great detail while almost nothing is saved of his childhood. The one exception is the story in the Gospel of Luke of his becoming separated from his parents at 12 years old because he lingered too long with rabbis in the temple in Jerusalem.

Both liberals and conservatives err by counting upon "historical accuracy" as a basis for faith. Liberals tend to discount the miraculous because it cannot be scientifically proven and conservatives claim the Bible is completely and absolutely scientifically true. Both miss the point: Matters of faith are not submissive to science. What matters is the experience of healing and transformation in the heart of the believer, although this is nurtured in the context of a historical tradition.

While the Bible has generally stood the test of historical accuracy with regard to the life of Jesus, believers must accept the reality that almost all of what we know of him is from the believer's interpretive account.

You may question my faith based upon such shaky historical ground. Yet I wonder why anyone who claims to know the resurrected Jesus would need to apply the historical, scientific method of today to an ancient time in order to believe.

Is there such a place as Hell?
Where does Satan live, and where do people go who don't
love God? (from a children's Sunday School class)

Hell and damnation are spoken of frequently in Christian scripture, including the teachings of Jesus (as in Matthew 11:23). Some churches include a doctrine of Hell as a place of eternal punishment, based upon such passages of scripture understood literally.

The idea of a place where souls are tortured forever has been seen by many Christians, however, to be in conflict with the main thrust of Jesus' teaching and his invitation to join the heavenly banquet. They stress the grace of God, God's readiness to forgive and Christ's defeat of evil.

Personally, I believe the words of Jesus in Matthew 9:2 to be the final word: "Take heart, my son; your sins are forgiven." This is the core of his teaching and life. Some of his last words from the cross, according to Luke, were "Father, forgive them for they know not what they do."

The idea of Hell as a tormented abode of the dead comes late in Hebrew tradition, during the time period just before Jesus' birth. Jesus capitalized on the symbolism of Hell perhaps to stress the urgency of people's need to repent and receive his message. The point is that God's love is not forced upon us. Yet not to enjoy it is the worst state imaginable. God invites us, and of course always loves us, but love must be responded to in order to be enjoyed.

While we do not know exactly what Heaven will be like, we know from our experience of God's love in this life that it will be wonderful, and that in many ways, it has already begun for those who know the unconditional love of God.

But what of those who do not accept? Here we need to be extremely cautious. It is not for us to judge others' state of heart and mind, not to mention their soul. Further, we cannot limit the grace of God to the means through which we have experienced it. How do we know Christ will not find other ways to communicate his love to those who don't know him when the church, somehow, has failed? Jesus describes his mission, after all, as one of a shepherd seeking his lost sheep.

Certainly the church has not been a perfect vessel of grace. Will God reject those who have rejected Christ because of the abuse of Christians? Of course not.

The Christian scriptures describe Jesus as descending into Hell to preach to the dead. While the meaning of this may be obscure, one possibility is that Jesus finds a way, through his own death, to speak to those who have not known him as their personal Lord and Savior in this life. Even after death, Jesus does not give up on us.

It is unwise to be too dogmatic about what happens after we die. We can only speak with symbols, because we cannot know what our existence will be like. If we trust Jesus, we know that our life has meaning and purpose for God, and that God's love for us guarantees that we will not be swept away into nothingness or condemned to eternal damnation.

Evil will one day not exist. This is hard for us to imagine, but it is the sense of the Bible that evil has already been defeated by the love of God and that there is no ultimate place for it in God's kingdom. The idea of hell as a place of eternal suffering ruled by Satan is irreconcilable with the sovereignty of the God we know in Jesus and Hebrew tradition.

I find the Psalms troubling. I love their beauty and passion for God, but just as I become involved in that part, I begin to read hateful things toward others. For example, Psalm 55 contains these words: "Let death come upon them; let them go down alive to Sheol; for evil is in their homes and in their hearts." Why are the Psalms so filled with hatred?

Indeed, the Psalms are full of passion and their frankness is remarkable. Magnificent as poetic hymns of anger and loneliness as well as praise and adoration, they help us to get in touch with the fullness of our humanity.

The Psalms reveal that anger is part of being human. If you have trouble accepting the bitter resentment and desire for revenge which is evident in some of the Psalms, you may be out of touch with such feelings within yourself. The danger lies not with the feeling of anger itself, but with our inability to deal with anger in healthy ways.

For instance, Psalm 55 is poignantly therapeutic for one who has been betrayed in a relationship with a friend, lover, or spouse. Anger is real at such times, no matter how much one may wish to suppress, rationalize, or forgive. The Psalm speaks the words we can scarcely say. "My heart is in anguish within me, the terrors of death have fallen upon me...horror overwhelms me...It is not enemies who taunt me - I could bear that; but it is you, my equal, my companion, my familiar friend, with whom I kept pleasant company; we walked in the house of God with the throng...My companion laid hands on a friend and violated a covenant with me with speech smoother than butter, but with a heart set on war; with words that were softer than oil, but in fact were drawn swords...You, O God, will cast them down into the lowest pit; the bloodthirsty and treacherous shall not live out half their days. But I will trust in you."

Unresolved anger lies at the core of much human suffering. The Psalms invite us to make our peace with anger by holding it up as a mirror. But we reject the invitation for several reasons.

First, anger frightens us. Our passions are always a little frightening because they push us to the fringes of self-control. We are afraid of what we might do if we acted from our anger. There are times we wish others harm, even someone we love. Psalm 55 invites us to acknowledge the truth about our anger while trusting God to take the appropriate measures to make things right.

Second, anger violates our high opinion of ourselves. We are taught from a very young age that feeling anger is unacceptable. Yet, anger is a natural product of the normal socialization process through which we learn that we are not the center of the universe. Knowledge begins to rule our emotions. We also learn that anger is unacceptable from people who are themselves afraid of normal expressions of anger. Perhaps they have been subjected to others whose anger was expressed in abusive ways. Overall, we learn that there is little place for anger in happy families or civilized society. Our value system does not legitimize anger for fear that it might be acted upon. And we are shocked to see it in the Bible.

When something happens which makes us angry, our knowledge intervenes to check our feelings. Sadly, such anger is often directed inward for lack of appropriate expression.

Finally, feelings of anger violate our understanding of Christian faith. We are taught to forgive. The fact is, however, that forgiveness cannot begin to be truly felt until one acknowledges deep feelings of betrayal. God's forgiveness begins with grace, but our forgiveness of others begins with repentance. Once we acknowledge our anger, and I mean in the fullness of our rage and desire for revenge, only then can we place it on the altar of our faith. For the light of God's forgiveness to enter us, we must open the door to the dark feelings which we quite naturally have.

This is not to say that anger is a negative thing. On the contrary, anger serves to help mold our individual identity in formative years and motivates us to respond to evil in the world in our adult lives. It is our refusal to look at our anger which is negative. God invites us through the Psalms to do that.

In Matthew 23:9 Jesus says, "And call no man your father upon the earth: for one is your Father, which is in heaven." Why, then, do you and some other members of the clergy refer to yourselves as father? Aren't you violating Jesus' instruction?

In the passage you quote, I believe Jesus meant that no one should take the place of God. Churches which call male clergy "father" obviously believe that Jesus did not mean his teaching to be taken legalistically. If so, we would not even refer to our biological fathers thusly. Nor would we call anyone "teacher," "rabbi," or "leader" because Jesus mentioned these in the same passage. Ironically, those who take issue with the reference to "father" have no problem referring to their clergy as "pastor," or "reverend."

Jesus did not intend to remove family words from our vocabulary, but to place such relationships in their appropriate context. Each of us has a relationship with God which is intended to be our primary influence. God is our ultimate parent, teacher, pastor, and friend. In placing God as the center of our value system, we choose God's values over the values of the world. It is in this sense that only God is our parent and teacher.

Your question raises the issue of authority. Are decisions a matter of personal conscience or are they based on the teaching of our elders through church tradition? Do we have a responsibility to discern the will of God for our lives by struggling with important matters in prayer, working out our own salvation in fear and trembling? Or, can we simply refer to the teaching of our religious tradition for the answers to life's important questions?

The dominant model in Christianity has been hierarchical. In this model ultimate authority comes from outside the believer rather than from the believer's own internal and personal relationship with God. Another model might be called the mystical. This is when authority comes from the individual believer's own sense of God's revelation. Both models are vital to the Christian faith, and we all live in tension between our individual conscience and the values of the faith community.

When one gives one's heart to Christ, there can be no other ultimate allegiance. While church tradition becomes one of the ways a believer may know and grow in Christ, the mystical model suggests that the authority of the church is useful, but not final. The hierarchical model, on the other hand, suggests that the authority of personal faith must be validated by the teaching of the church. Thus, the mystical model is always in tension with and sometimes confrontational with the hierarchical model. Ideally, hierarchical structures do not become abusive, and individuals remain humble in their willingness to learn from and contribute to the larger tradition.

The practice of calling priests father is derived from the principle that the Church is the "family of God." Now that women are ordained as priests in some churches, they may appropriately be called "mother," although most women clergy I know prefer not to use this term.

While I refer to myself as "Father Hansen," I am ambivalent about it. First, it is too hierarchical. To refer to a church officer as father implies that the church members are children. The use of "father" may be subtly disabling of the laity, perpetuating patriarchal dominance of the church in an age when women are able to take their place along side men as priests and secular leaders.

Second, the use of "father" includes the risk of setting the church apart from those who are not in the "family." Church history is dominated by a "we/they" mentality which has diminished the dignity of those who were not "in the fold." This is the very perspective which Jesus confronted in the religious community of his own day when he argued with the Pharisees who preferred to separate themselves from outsiders. From Jesus' perspective, no one is an outsider. If the church considers itself a family, then it must include all of humanity in that family, which of course, it typically does not do.

Finally, "father" is problematic for me because most women clergy do not wish to be called "mother." Men and women are partners in church leadership, and the terminology must express such a partnership. Without the cooperation of women priests willing to be called "mother", referring to men as "father" must come to an end. As more women take their place beside men in important church positions, clarity will emerge, at least for me, on this question. Until then, call me a traditionalist!

The Bible tells of God giving the Holy Land to the Jews by telling them to slaughter the people who were already living there. Slaughter is still going on in the Holy Land in the name of God. How can a loving God order such things? And if it was not God who ordered it, as recorded, then how can the Bible be considered to be inspired?

You have put your finger on the most troublesome part of the Bible for many, the conquering of the Promised Land by the Hebrew people. Readers can find the stories of massacre and bloodshed in the books of Joshua and I & II Samuel. These stories cannot be reconciled with a God who loves all of humanity. Nor can they be reconciled with the God we know through the ministry of Jesus Christ.

History is written by the victors. The Hebrew stories of conquering the Promised Land were written from a biased human point of view, not God's. The nomadic tribes of Jacob's descendants, led by Joshua, successfully invaded that part of the world we now call the Holy Land.

After some initial victories against overwhelming odds, they settled into a long period of unstable rule, first under judges, and later under their own kings. Trouble was constantly present from within and without the Hebrew nation until it divided itself into northern and southern kingdoms, and eventually was conquered by the Babylonians.

Out of this history a theological understanding of God evolved. "If we obey God's commandments explicitly, God will miraculously help us to conquer our enemies. To the degree that we are disobedient, God will use our enemies to punish us. Punishment is not pleasing to God, but has the effect of bringing us back to obedience and blessing." This is the theology expressed in the part of the Bible to which you refer.

It is better to obey God's plan for us than to disobey. This is the inspired message contained in the uninspired context of one people attempting to obliterate another. These stories are important to the overall revelation of scripture not only for the truths they contain, but also for the lessons we learn from their excessive claims to God's partiality.

One needs to read the whole Bible, including other Hebrew texts and particularly the words of Jesus in the Gospels, in order to place the conquering narratives in their appropriate context.

There is a counter-theology in the Hebrew scriptures which one finds in Ruth, Jonah, the Suffering Servant passages in Isaiah, and elsewhere. In these places we find God caring for all of humanity and valuing what other non-Hebrew people have to offer as God's chosen instruments.

Jesus, of course, lived a life of non-violence and taught his followers to do likewise. Some will argue that by upsetting tables in the temple he was being violent, but he was angrily making room for the Gentiles' place which had been co-opted by the merchants. Jesus' expression of anger at this exclusion is hardly a sanction for bloodshed.

Jesus confronted the theology which says that God is biased toward one people. He also confronted the theology which says that people suffer in this world because of God's punishment in response to their sins, as we see in Luke 13:2. Sadly, we Christians today are heard to replace obedience with the faith of our traditions as God's standard for acceptance.

We wrongly assume that God is on our side alone and will punish unbelievers. However, the theology of grace makes no such claims. It simply says that obedience is not the criteria which God uses to judge us. Rather, we are already judged in Christ, who died for our sins, and not for ours only, but for the sins of everyone (1 John 2:2)

God's grace is intended to evoke a response from us, which is faith. Faith makes a difference, hopefully, in the lives of Christians. But faith is not a call to prejudice. Rather, faith calls us to servanthood without partiality. By our witness to the love of God for all humanity we are faithful to our Lord.

The shops are full of objects depicting angels - jewelry, greeting cards, books, dresser trays, pictures, etc. There's even a TV special on the subject. What is your theological opinion on the existence of angels, personal guardian angels, and what appears to be a cult centered on angels?

The Epistle entitled Hebrews says a lot to me about the Christian perspective on angels. In Chapter 1, the author offers an extended comparison between the angels and Jesus Christ, closing the chapter with this sentence: "Are not all angels spirits in the divine service, sent to serve for the sake of those who are to inherit salvation?"

This passage draws from the many biblical stories of angels serving as messengers of God's activity, blessing, and good news. It underscores the idea that they serve the purposes of God as they minister to humanity. Angels are not human beings who have gone to heaven, a popular misconception. They are unique creatures of God who carry God's love to us. Scripture and tradition also reveal that angels have a volitional nature. Like human beings, they can choose whether to fulfill their calling or to betray it. Supernatural spirits who oppose the will of God are considered "fallen angels" and constitute the legion of demons whose lord is not Jesus Christ, but Satan. We see this especially in apocalyptic literature, although such literature (Revelation, e.g.) uses angel imagery to disguise very human persons who were the persecutors of the faithful.

While Christian tradition affirms the ministry of angels, and religious art is resplendent with them, the subject has not been taken too seriously, I believe, for two reasons. First, it has been revealed to us in scripture that some angels, at least, disobey God. This places us at a disadvantage with regard to any "relationship" with angels. How do we know when an angel is serving our Lord Jesus Christ or the forces opposed to God? Why would we want to open ourselves to deception and risk our well-being? The ambivalence in scripture toward angels ought to give us pause in our fascination with them.

Second, and more important, why would we want to seek the blessings of angels when we have the very presence of God our Savior within us? A serious devotion to angels gives priority to the messengers rather than to the One who sends the message.

In this regard, we need to remember an important spiritual principle: Know the difference between academic interest and devotional interest. Do you believe in angels? If you say yes, what do you mean? Do you simply believe in their existence and you are interested to learn more about them? Then your interest is harmless and can even be helpful in the understanding of your faith in God. If, however, you mean that you trust in the powers of angels quite apart from or instead of a meaningful relationship with God, then your interest is devotional and you are placing your ultimate good in the wrong hands.

I sometimes think the angels must be embarrassed by all of the attention they have been receiving lately. Good angels know that they have only accomplished their mission if they succeed in strengthening our faith in the one true God who is the creator of us all.

I have stopped attending my Bible study because people there jump on everything I say. I feel attacked and unaccepted. I want to study the Bible, but I'm not up to having to defend every thought I have. Have any suggestions?

There are basically two approaches to Bible study. The first views the Bible as a treasure map. Directions need to be followed explicitly or the treasure will not be found. There is no room for more than one correct interpretation. The second views the Bible somewhat like a telephone. By studying the Bible in faith, one enters a unique conversation with God. Because of the personal relationship God extends to each of us, each will find inspiration according to his or her own personality and gifts. Each will contribute to the richness of group study by sharing those conversations with God.

While the treasure map analogy avers that each person conform to the Bible's message narrowly admonished by the faith community, the telephone analogy holds that each person brings the Biblical message to life through individual inspiration as nurtured within that faith community. The treasure map demands compliance. The telephone demands responsibility, integrity, and humility.

You are a person who wants to be respected for your ideas and find acceptance as you struggle with your own relationship with God. You may have to find a Bible study which suits your needs. There are many faith communities in your area like that.

A Bible study which encourages individual interpretation and expression does not guarantee, of course, that there will not be individuals who are threatened by ideas other than their own and "jump on" others. A wise and assertive leader will notice this when it happens and prevent it. Lacking that, there are some things you can do which apply not only to Bible study, but to any situation when your ideas are attacked.

First, remember your identity. You are a child of God and your connection with the Holy Spirit is just as powerful as anyone else's. None of us has only a little piece of God in our hearts. Rather, God's gift is to be present with us through faith. This is the meaning of Jeremiah 31:33,34: "I will put my law within them and write it on their hearts. I will be their God, and they will be my people. None of them will have to teach his fellow countryman to know the Lord, because all will know me, from the least to the greatest."

Remind yourself that your knowledge of God is as valid as the person's attacking you. If you are secure in that knowledge, you will not feel vulnerable.

Second, know that when someone attacks you it is not about you, but about them. Try not to be threatened by the argument. Instead of allowing them to break through your sense of self, listen to what they are saying for what it reveals not only about God but about them. Focusing on the other person rather than yourself will help you to be less vulnerable and more objective.

Third, try to respond rather than to react. Because you are clear about your right to your viewpoint, you can respond to the comment without the emotions of fear, personal hurt, or anger. Psychologists call this "managing one's own reactivity." Acquiring this skill will prevent personalities coming into play and increase your ability to focus upon the issue of the discussion.

Murray Bowen, in Family Therapy in Clinical Practice, states the goal in three rules: "Don't attack, don't defend, and don't withdraw." This is called "differentiated functioning." Readers may write to me for more information and resources on the subject.

God calls people of faith to take personal and often courageous positions on biblical material. We are also called to relate to others thoughtfully, resolving our differences, if necessary, in a climate of mutual respect.

The Kingdom of God is not a matter of finding the map to heaven and conforming to it. Rather, it is knowing God and loving one another as we are loved.

WORSHIP

I had a friend ask me recently why I went to church. All I could think to say was, "Because I couldn't get through the week without it." I wish I could have said more. What would you say?

I think you gave a wonderful response. It was a personal witness to the meaning and strength you receive from corporate worship. The following are some of the reasons you and many others find regular church attendance to have great value.

Worship reminds us of who we are. We receive many messages in the world each day. Many gods make their claim upon us and seek to give us an identity which is not the one given by the one true God who loves us unconditionally. Remembering with those who worship God, while from many perspectives, helps us, literally, to remember our true identity.

You express some struggle in getting through the week. Most of us can relate to this sense of feeling drained by the demands of family, friends, and work, and the desire to improve ourselves. These are all desirable in life, but they can also make inappropriate claims upon us which can be unhealthy for us.

Through worship, God gives us a healthy perspective, heals, and renews us. If we never took our car in for service, it wouldn't operate properly very long. Worship is like that, but even more, it's as though when we first take our car in, its a rundown cheap model, and each time it is given back to us upgraded to a more expensive model in better condition. After a while, we're driving a fine Rolls Royce. Without regular worship, we run the risk of losing sight of the meaning and purpose of our existence. With regular worship, we are gradually transformed into a child of God.

This transformation process is not magical of course. It is the product of a sincere struggle with our faith in God and the lessons we learn from relationships. Ideally, churches are not homogenous communities, but places where we can rub shoulders with those who are different from ourselves. Through the obvious tension of such relationships, we learn to open ourselves to the mystery of God's creation and the message of God's acceptance.

There is an unfortunate tendency in human nature to move toward like-mindedness with others and become fortresses against the world. Churches sometimes do this rather than becoming welcoming communities who seek ways to engage the world. When this happens, the traditions of an increasingly isolated community become reinforced and, while it may make converts of others, it is not itself in the process of growing in holiness.

We need to find a community which will nurture our spiritual growth while accepting our uniqueness. In such a context we can learn to trust and become the person God created us to be.

When we are part of such a worshipping community we can make a greater difference in the world around us. Not only do we learn to serve God by becoming stronger in our faith, but together with others, we are more effective than we are alone. Thus, in our own individual ways, we help our church to be a place where others seeking God can come also.

We help our church to meet the needs of the hungry and the homeless. We provide spiritual education and fellowship for young people. We provide clergy who teach and provide pastoral care for individuals and families in crisis. We provide those worship opportunities through which we are able to lose ourselves in order to find our true selves. In short, we make a central place of God in the midst of a world which otherwise would make no place for God.

It is certainly true that one can have a relationship with God without going to church, but anyone who seriously wants such a relationship would be wise to seek the nourishment of church experiences. They would soon find, like yourself, that they couldn't get through the week without it.

*Would you explain why pag-
eantry and ritual are necessary to worship God? To
me, it seems like a lot of "hocus pocus."*

Pageantry and ritual are not necessary. God is less concerned
with the style of worship than with the attitude. Worship pleasing to God always contains one essential ingredient: hearts which
are offered and open.

Jesus quotes Isaiah in Mark 7:6, "This people honors me with
their lips, but their hearts are far from me; in vain do they worship
me, teaching human precept as doctrines." Jesus was revealing
hypocrisy in the actions of his listeners, a slightly different subject, but his reference does remind us that God wants our hearts.
This is why the ancient celebration of the Holy Eucharist, or Mass,
always begins with the Sursum Corda, or "Lift up your hearts."

Styles of worship are always intended as an offering to God.
To the degree that worship edifies the people of God and strengthens us in our faith it accomplishes its purpose. While pageantry
and ritual are not necessary, they can be edifying.

It is important to understand that corporate worship is about
telling a story. We learn the faith passed down to us by the stories
told in the community of faith. They are recorded in the Bible, of
course, and they are also recorded in the liturgy of the church. The
reason for ritual is primarily to protect the integrity of the story.
Regardless of the inherent ability of the minister to communicate
the story, it will be told in the ritual. The story will be what the
larger church believes, not simply the personal version of the minister.

Christian liturgy takes the revelation of the Bible and sum-
marizes it in the prayers and creeds of worship. Through such
worship we are connected to the faith of our ancestors and the larger
body of believers in the world today.

Beyond its protective value, ritual makes available the best
worship of the church over the centuries. Some beautiful and meaningful prayers of saints have become part of contemporary worship. We participate in the magnificence of their spirituality when
we share their prayers, not in a rote way, but genuinely with our
hearts lifted to God. There is a degree of quality control as well as

warranty protection because of ritual.

With regard to pageantry, I can understand how this might seem foolish to some. But think of it this way. Symbols can be powerful communicators. The story is told not only with words, but with signs and movements. Artistic expression communicates beyond words, and can stir the soul very deeply. Liturgical worship seeks to engage the whole person. You might say the words speak to the left side of the brain and pageantry and ceremony speak to the right side.

Both are important receivers, not only of a message, but even more important, of God's presence. All of the pageantry which may surround a celebration of the Holy Eucharist, for example, is intended to enliven the experience of God through the act of receiving Communion. All sacraments consist of both words and symbols.

There is also something to be said for offering God our best. Yes, we could feed lots of people for what a silver chalice costs, but would we? Can we not acknowledge the preciousness of the act of worship with appropriate vessels and find other ways to economize in our lives in order to feed the hungry?

We may be critical of precious things in worship while enjoying precious things for our own use. Is this not putting ourselves before God? People of faith have always offered God the best of what they can produce. This expresses their desire to place God first in their lives.

Pageantry and ceremony always mark the highest moments in the collective life of a community. There is no moment higher than that of returning thanks to God who gives us our very lives.

I have a problem with the teaching of my priest that we should be quiet in church. Isn't it more important to be friendly than quiet?

You must be from a church that values the importance of liturgy. Generally speaking such churches teach that the environment of worship should not be social, but reverent.

Certainly any church ought to be a friendly place. Making people feel welcome in a sincere environment of caring is an impor-

tant function of religious communities. In the church building itself, however, the focus of the community is upon God rather than
upon one another. Liturgical churches conspire through the arts of
architecture, ceremony, ritual and music to create a sense of the
holy in our lives. The worship setting is intended to be a spiritual
oasis in the midst of a world of distraction and confusion.

Episcopal bishop James A. Pike, controversial as he was during the 1950s, was a great advocate of the traditional silence within
the church prior to and following corporate worship. In his book,
Beyond Anxiety, he refers to a passage from Isaiah, "They that wait
upon the Lord shall renew their strength." He said, "This is one of
three roles of public worship - to provide a special atmosphere in
which it is more possible to sense the reality of the living God."

We are rarely quiet in our busy lives. Yet, there is nothing
more helpful in combating stress or gaining perspective than taking the time to simply be - without doing anything. I don't need to
extol the value of meditation or prayer, and there is no better place
for these disciplines than in the church. The sanctuary of the church
is set apart from the rest of the world as a place of prayer.

There are other rooms for fellowship, meals and education.
The church is a different place, a little space to sense heaven on
earth. The church is holy ground and reminds us that God is present
everywhere. "The Lord is in his holy temple: let all the earth keep
silence before him."

To be silent in the midst of the company of friend and stranger
is actually very friendly. By doing so we confess to one another
that we all share a common heritage, the loving presence of God.
We give a gift to one another by honoring the silence. We know
that while words may not be spoken aloud, there are many conversations going on between people and their God.

But the primary purpose of the silence is not out of respect
for others, but for the company of God. The silence highlights the
importance of the occasion of worship. It is not that God is present
in the church and nowhere else. Rather, it is the realization that
when we enter a church to pray, we are entering a space in our
lives and the lives of others which is truly holy.

Churches are made holy by the intentions of people's hearts
given to God. Reverence for God demands that we suspend our secu-

lar niceties and together prepare ourselves to listen to God speaking to us.

I once was walking down a sidewalk in a major city and encountered a street musician performing wonderful classical music on a cello. The grace and beauty of it put me in awe, and all I could do was stop and listen. My heart was lifted and my soul nourished by the beauty of the moment.

At first, it was as though the musician and I were the only people in all of creation. Gradually, I began to realize that scores of people were passing by - talking, laughing, or striding as though harnessed like a team of horses racing to its destination. At first, I thought, how rude. Then I thought, how sad that they were not having the experience I was.

When we enter a church, we are saying that we want to allow the music of God's loving presence to enfold us. It's a time to silence the ordinary and let the extraordinary heal and transform us. We need those sacred places desperately in our busy world. Through them God can nurture the sacred place within us.

Would you explain the Episcopal Church's basic beliefs and practices?

I'm always happy to talk about that which I love. Since you asked, here goes. My first thought is that if you have been a regular reader of my column, you already know a great deal about the Episcopal Church. I never speak for the church, of course, but I am a product of it.

What cannot be seen in the column is the great liturgy of the church. There is a certain ritual and ceremony contained in the Book of Common Prayer which allows the people to be involved in corporate worship, not only as individuals, but as people of God. Episcopal worship engages the whole person and the whole congregation in a corporate expression of the adoration of God. And, congregations around the globe in the Anglican Communion are joined together in the sacred traditions and truths of worship which trace their history to the earliest days of Christianity. In this respect the Episcopal Church considers itself to be catholic, i.e., one with the church everywhere and at all times.

Because we are united by a common liturgy, the Episcopal Church has not found the need to create unity with dogmatic statements of faith. We hold as our doctrine only the ancient Trinitarian creeds of the once-united church because we feel that any further doctrinal statements only serve to divide the Body of Christ. The result of this refusal to establish a "confession" for the Episcopal Church is a great tolerance for, even a desire for, diversity of viewpoints in every conceivable matter. Decisions by the national church represent both the clergy and laity, and give a sense of where the church stands, but are not imposed upon everyone. The church can be said to be pastoral rather than hierarchical and authoritarian. One worships with people with whom one profoundly disagrees, hopefully recognizing that we all answer to God and can learn from one another.

Freedom from dogma equips our church with a sense of pilgrimage. We don't have all the answers, but we know we walk with Christ, who is leading us into the future. There is a felt sense of wonder and awe in the Episcopal Church. From our great cathedrals to the little mission in the village, the church embodies in architecture and congregational life a sense of the Holy. We consider it as important to preserve the mystery as to define the truth.

Tolerance of varied viewpoints implies that the Episcopal Church is an inclusive church, and at our best we are. Yet, it is not an easy church to belong to. The church expects a lot of its members by not making it clear what one has to do to be a "good Episcopalian." The church nurtures the process of discernment without offering simplistic answers. It is always more difficult to discern God's voice from within than to be told what God is saying. The love of Christ is always our guide, but it is not always clear what love commands.

The Episcopal Church affirms creation as the means of God's grace. We are not quick to condemn that which is not of our tradition because we believe in the inherent goodness of all things. It is not so much what a thing is, but how it is used as to where judgment is placed. The church is therefore open to truth revealed through science, other religions, the arts, and anywhere else in creation.

The Episcopal Church does not mold people into uniformity,

but nurtures them to take their place in the glorious tapestry of God's kingdom. Ironically, if you visit an Episcopal Church, you may feel you are led to conformity by the liturgy. But remember, common worship allows for a rich diversity of uncommon people.

> *What's wrong with modern Episcopalianism allowing the use and teaching of the 1928 Book of Common Prayer? It seems to me that the church has opened its mind so far as to swing around shut from the other direction.*

I thank the reader for sending this "in-house" question, and trust that regular readers, only about two percent of whom are Episcopalians, will find something of value nonetheless.

Your question requires laying some groundwork. First, the Book of Common Prayer (BCP) contains worship and historical documents which represent the faith and tradition of the Episcopal Church. It is based upon the Bible and draws from the best of church tradition as it sets forth worship for our day.

Every fifty years or so, the Prayer Book is revised in order to utilize the advantage of hindsight. It is partly a process of correcting undue influences in former revisions, and also of making the BCP relevant to our contemporary experience of God and life. The BCP is more important for Episcopalians than some other books of worship might be for other denominations because the Episcopal Church finds its unity through worship rather than doctrine.

While the Church is orthodox in its Christianity (i.e., Trinitarian), we have not developed doctrines which might divide us from the rest of Christianity. Our unity with all of Christianity and our respect for the dignity of other faiths is central to our witness of the love and truth of Jesus Christ.

Where there is great tolerance for diversity of belief, there needs to be a common worship holding us together. We derive from the worship our connection to the earliest church, the best of the church through the ages, and unity with the Anglican Communion throughout the world.

There is another sense in which "Common" is understood. The Episcopal Church has always held that worship must be in the "language of the people." This was strongly felt during the Reformation when the Latin of Roman Catholic worship was experienced as dominance of the Roman hierarchy by reformers. If people worship with language which they do not speak on a daily basis, it is not truly their own worship. At best it is "sacred language." At worst, it is the language of those in power.

The language of the Bible was common language in both the Hebrew and Greek Testaments. The Episcopal Church tries to keep the language at its contemporary best while remaining true to the tradition. One might argue whether we succeed at this, but one cannot argue for tradition simply by clinging to one moment in the tradition, as in this case, the 1928 BCP.

Your question alleges that there is antipathy toward 1928 Prayer Book Episcopalians. If so, I'm not aware of it, unless you interpret the principles I've outlined above as being antipathetic. "Freedom of Choice" in worship is discouraged in the Episcopal Church because our worship says who we are and what we share. We believe what we pray.

As an Episcopal priest, for example, I am bound to use the BCP and the scriptures appointed for certain days. This protects the church from my own preferences and idiosyncrasies. People in the pew may not be fed by the words of my sermon, but they will surely be fed by the liturgy of the church.

My experience has been that there is a great deal of respect and appreciation of those who wish to remain with the 1928 Prayer Book. While the church cannot officially have more than one BCP, it has been very pastoral in its effort to keep 1928'ers in the fold. The newest BCP contains forms using traditional language, and most bishops tolerate use of the 1928 Book. Such acceptance and tolerance is not apparent toward the new BCP by "28ers."

I would hope that, in any case, these controversies not become personal. But in truth, they have at times.

*Why do people cross themselves? I
have a friend who crosses herself whenever she hears of
a death. Once I saw someone cross himself when he
walked in front of a church. Usually, though, I see it at
weddings and funerals when the priest gives the blessing. What does it mean?*

To cross one's self is simply to become wholly mindful of one's
identity in Jesus Christ. This simple act of devotion recalls
the gift of salvation received sacramentally at baptism and reminds
us that we are children of God.

The cross is a symbol of Christian hope and trust in God's
love. Making the sign of the cross on our bodies is to "cover" ourselves in Jesus Christ. Crossing is used in the catholic traditions,
Roman, Orthodox and Anglican. These historic churches engage
the body both in corporate liturgy and personal devotions.

To stand, bow, kneel and genuflect are some of the ways the
body is used. Churches of these traditions tend to be ornate archi-
tecturally, which engages the eye. And they often use incense, which
engages the nose.

But back to crossing. It is a kind of wordless prayer. Your
friend who crosses herself at the mention of someone dying is saying, perhaps, "May this person be received into heaven according
to God's mercy in Christ." Christians believe that we are saved not
by our good deeds but by the love of God made manifest in Jesus.
To cross is to claim that love for whomever is on our heart.

As for the person who might cross himself passing a church,
this is an extreme expression of the custom of reverencing the presence of God when inside a church. When one passes in front of the
altar, some form of acknowledgment of God is made, usually a slight
bow. While we are aware of God's presence everywhere, the altar
is the liturgical symbol of that reality. To acknowledge God there
is to acknowledge God in all places.

You will also see people dipping their fingers in Holy Water,
when provided, and then crossing themselves upon entering or leaving a church. Holy Water is water which has been used for baptism, and is therefore blessed in the context of the sacrament of
God's gift of salvation. When entering the church the sign of the

cross with Holy Water says, "I am placing myself in the hands of a God who loves me unconditionally and I want to be open to God's nurture and call through worship." When leaving the church it means, "I go forth knowing that I possess gifts of the Holy Spirit for ministry in the name of Jesus Christ, and that I am called to that ministry."

Other common appropriate moments for crossing oneself are when receiving Communion, saying thanks at meals, and saying your prayers. It is a simple way of centering as you commune with God. There is always the danger that simple acts of devotion can be done mindlessly out of habit. Or, they may be done because everyone else is doing it, and the meaning is not understood. We need to know that such practices are not obligatory, but edifying if done from the heart with thankful intention.

I personally enjoy the tangible simplicity of such customs. We tend to intellectualize our faith, and these body activities remind us that faith is not so much a matter of understanding as doing. The acts themselves do not answer fully God's call to us, but they can help us to be appropriately focused on the love of God.

I encourage you to develop some such physical aspect in your devotions to God. Actions do speak louder than words, and they affirm the body as a means of God's grace.

> *I haven't been to church in awhile, and I am in the crossroads of my life at the age of 23. I would like to strengthen my faith in religion, but all the churches in the college are too social. Is it O.K. to watch services on TV, or does one have to enter a church? Could you please give me some advice on my situation?*

Many people say, "I'm a Christian", who never attend church. So you are not alone. Because God is everywhere, there is no reason why you cannot be strengthened in your faith by observing a service or listening to an evangelist on TV. I have known people who in the privacy of their home, or even in a motel room while traveling, have had profound spiritual experiences. As Jesus said to Nicodemus, "The wind blows where it chooses."

Faith in Jesus Christ will eventually move one into community, however. While people can have spiritual experiences in any context, if such encounters become important in their lives, they will seek others who have had similar urgings in order to understand, grow, and share what God has given to them.

The Judeo-Christian tradition is particularly one of participation in the faith of the community as opposed to individual enlightenment. The religious community, imperfect as it is, is nonetheless the bearer of the faith through history. It nurtures the faith through its rituals and writings. And, it offers challenge and support for ministry.

It is not an exaggeration to say that Christian faith is by definition participation in a community which seeks to worship and serve Jesus Christ. Each person's relationship with Christ is personal, to be sure, but each person is accountable to Christian doctrine, Holy Scripture, and pastoral leadership if they wish to call themselves Christian.

My advice to you, therefore, is to find a community which will nurture you. It should be more than a place where you feel comfortable, although that is important. It should also be a place which respects the spirituality of each person, helps to nurture your relationship with Christ, and challenges you by helping you to see Christ in people who may be quite different from yourself.

Faith seldom matures in isolation from others. Life's experiences need to be brought to our relationship with God, and our relationship with God needs to be brought to our relationship with people.

In the First Epistle of John we are told, "Those who say, 'I love God' and hate their brothers or sisters are liars; for those who do not love a brother or sister whom they have seen, cannot love God whom they have not seen." There is, therefore, an important connection between our experience of God and the quality of our relationships with other people. The church knows this, and exists for the sole purpose of strengthening relationships with God and neighbor. This is what Christians are called to do, especially when such relationships are difficult or even broken altogether.

You sound hesitant to become involved in a church. You may have had experiences which make you cautious. Try to distinguish between what are truly abusive experiences from church communities and your own false expectations of people who belong to a church. People can be abusive, and they sometimes congregate in the name of God. But this does not characterize all churches. More often than not, we simply expect a church to consist of people who will always act lovingly toward us, and when they don't, we are disillusioned.

Think of your church community as a little laboratory in which you can learn to forgive the offenses of others, respect the diversity of God's gifts, learn to handle conflict in ways in which there are not winners and losers, and work together to build love, mutual respect, and compassion in your wider community.

If Christian faith is being reconciled with God in Christ, then its manifestation in our lives is reconciliation with one another. I don't think you can do that in front of a TV where nothing is asked of you except a donation. God wants more than that, and God has much more to offer.

> *Every year during Lent I give up something I enjoy with the intention of becoming closer to God. Some years I've been successful in my abstinence, and I pat myself on the back, and other years I fail and feel guilty. Either way, I can't honestly say that I've done much to accomplish my goal - to be closer to God. Can you offer some Lenten counsel?*

Lent is a time set aside in the church year for self-examination of our relationship with God and the values upon which our lives are based. The idea of "giving up" something for Lent is that we practice a change in our lifestyle which reminds us that this is a special time to reflect and evaluate the course of our lives.

As your question implies, we often focus on the discipline we have adopted as the means of growing closer to God. It is trivial to think, however, that giving up chocolate would bring me closer to God! But it is not so trivial, when I am reaching for a chocolate, to remember that this is Lent, and that I have made a commitment to allow God to become more central in my life. The denial of the chocolate becomes the trigger which raises my consciousness and puts me back on course.

As you think about how you might grow closer to God during Lent, it might be helpful to know that there have been two traditional paths taken in the course of human spirituality.

One of these paths is the negative way. Eastern religions as well as Christianity have been dominated by the negative way, which stresses sacrifice, suffering and the denial of pleasure as the path toward a closer union with God. Strongly influenced by Greek philosophical categories, Christian asceticism has leaned toward a sense of the physical, particularly physical pleasure, as a lower order of existence. The goal of such asceticism is to become more spiritual by rejecting earthly comforts and pleasures.

The negative path reminds us that the created order is not God and should not be the ultimate basis for our value system. Giving up chocolates may help me to realize how attached I have become to them. The negative path strays from a Judeo-Christian expression of spirituality, however, when it denies the essential goodness of the physical order and diminishes a sense of appreciation and enjoyment of all which God has made.

The other path is called the positive way. This way stresses the physical realm as a means of Grace. The world is filled with opportunities to know and love God and neighbor. During Lent, people who wish to travel the positive way might decide to become more involved in a ministry, or take time to meditate upon and appreciate one's environment or family, or study the Bible or an important book which will help one to grow in knowledge and faith. The positive path strays from a Christian expression of spirituality when God's blessings are enjoyed with little or no acknowledgment of God, thanksgiving returned to God, or accountability for the use of creation according to God's purposes.

To say that one way is negative and the other positive does not imply that one is better than the other. They are both sides of the same coin of spirituality. The are both valuable and both contain the potential for being misused.

The fact that the negative way has dominated Christian spirituality, however, should not be taken lightly. Christians need to reclaim the goodness of creation, the holiness of being human in all of its fullness, and the connectedness of our humanity to God, to the earth, and to one another. These realities, while always present in Christian tradition, have been suppressed by institutions concerned more with order and the control of pleasure than with spontaneity and creativity.

Lent is the time to practice the art of knowing God in an intentional way. The discipline you adopt for Lent is not, in itself, your walk with God. The outward obedience to the discipline is much less important than the inward transformation which is sure to happen when you offer yourself more faithfully to God. Have a holy Lent!

My friend recently took me to her church where people were speaking in tongues. I've been a Christian all of my life and never encountered this before. Can you tell me why more churches don't practice it?

Tongues is one of the gifts of the Holy Spirit. As strange as tongues may be to those who are not familiar with it, it is a powerful experience for those to whom the gift is given. To be in the midst of a congregation where people are praising God in tongues, singing and speaking in beautiful, yet incomprehensible sounds which are usually very melodic, might be described by some as an experience of heaven, and by others as a bizarre nightmare.

Tongues has the tendency to be divisive, and was discouraged for public use by St. Paul. You can read how he felt about tongues in 1 Corinthians, Chapter 14. Aware of the fascination with the more dramatic gifts of the Spirit and how easy it is to forget our Lord's admonition to love one another, Paul would have us communicate the faith through sound teaching and good deeds.

His attitude is summarized by this statement, "In church, it is better to speak five words with my mind, in order to instruct others, than ten thousand words in a tongue."

This explains why many churches do not emphasize tongues, and may even discourage it. Yet, for those Christians who discover it, and for churches who teach about it, it becomes a central aspect of devotional and congregational life.

There are several settings in which tongues are used, and

they are, perhaps different gifts. One of these is in one's personal devotions. Here tongues is an intimate kind of communion with God which edifies one's faith. It is nothing less than the Spirit praying through us.

Another setting of tongues is in public worship where a tongue becomes a word of God to the people. A person may feel moved to speak out loud at a prayer meeting or corporate worship service. Paul taught that in this setting one should be sure that the gift of interpretation is present. The interpretation of tongues is another gift of the Spirit and is necessary to keep the worship intelligible. Finally, there is the setting for corporate prayer and praise, where people sing and speak in unison. This kind of public worship can be very uplifting and powerful.

Tongues should never be considered a litmus test for the presence of the Spirit. It is clear from Paul that it is the least of the gifts. He did not discourage tongues for individual use, but in terms of our service to others, it may do more harm than good.

A form of tongues was given to the apostles at the Feast of Pentecost. The Holy Spirit descended upon the apostles, and they began to preach the Good News in the languages of all the foreign peoples gathered together to celebrate Pentecost in Jerusalem. In this case, the gift of tongues was the ability to speak another's language. Perhaps this indicates why this phenomenon is given - to help us speak in God's language, the language of love. Everyone understands the language of love.

When we act for the good of another, we are using the most powerful tongue God has given. God's love breaks down all dividing lines of language, race and culture. The gift of tongues strengthens us in our experience of God's love for us, and to that end it is given.

EVANGELISM

Would you please offer some advice on evangelism? I just can't seem to find whatever it takes to share my faith with someone else.

You're in lots of company! Most people feel very uncomfortable telling others about their own relationship with God. And those who don't often seem to try to make others a carbon copy of themselves.

Evangelism, put simply, is passing on the Good News of God's love which you have received. It is not about making people members of your church or believers in a doctrine which you have been taught. It is not about words, but power, as St. Paul says. Evangelism is a way of being which manifests the qualities of God's presence within you and will, therefore, cause you to represent the love of God to others.

While evangelism is generally seen as "going forth," you might think of it as "being true." The going forth part happens automatically. We don't exist in a bubble. Our natural connections at home, in the work place, and elsewhere provide numerous daily encounters which are influenced by the quality of our relationship with God. We don't need to be missionaries in a foreign land to recognize the call to transform our daily lives by the love of God. The place to begin to think about evangelism, therefore, is with yourself.

The essential question one must ask is, "How loving am I, really?" For Christians, the quality of our love is assessed by the fruits of Christ's spirit. Galatians 5:22 is a good place to find a concise statement of what God's spirit received in Christ looks like: "...the fruit of the spirit is love, joy, peace, patience, kindness, generosity, faithfulness, gentleness, and self-control." To the degree that we possess these qualities we have the appropriate ingredients for evangelism. Too often pro-active evangelism, especially a program of evangelism, goes forth with ideas of doctrine and techniques of persuasion, with little regard for the embodiment of Christ's love.

If Christians first worked on the transformation of self before seeking to convert others, we would be far more fruitful in spreading the love of Christ. We would be free to love without conditions rather than driven by the agenda of our particular perspective. We would be emotionally and spiritually equipped to allow Christ to love through us rather than feeling the burden of thinking we must convert others to think as we do. We would know the difference between the love of God and the package which is intended to contain the love, but is not the love itself.

It might be said that we are all evangelists, whether we want to be or not. We cannot help making an impression. The real issue is the kind of an impression we make. If we want to transfer to others what we have, then we must truly have it. The impression must be truly Christ's face and not the face of our own historical and cultural situation. The wonderful thing about the love of God is that it is multi-colored. While the traditions of human beings are not easily shared between cultures, the love of God crosses all barriers. This is because God's spirit knows no boundaries and is not captured in any one expression of it, even the Judeo-Christian tradition. If we have not learned that from our tradition, then our tradition has become idolatrous.

Once you have begun to truly focus upon your own ability to love in Christ's name, then you are ready to take the next step. In a word, it is called servanthood. When you are unsure about what to say or what to do, simply pray for guidance in terms of what would be the kind and truly helpful thing, and then do it.

While we tend to think in categories of right and wrong in our behavior, Jesus invites us to think in terms of honoring and helping the other person. This goes far beyond being "nice." It also goes beyond trying to please. There are times when the kind and helpful thing is to say what a person does not want to hear. Evangelism is saying and doing what serves the good of others. When we can do that, we are the incarnate expression of Christ's love for them.

Would you please say more about evangelism as "being true?"

E vangelism begins not with "going forth," but with "being true." When we are able to be faithful to God's call to us to be loving people, sharing the Good News with others happens quite naturally in our homes, neighborhoods, and workplaces. To love is to be an evangelist. Without love, one cannot communicate the Gospel.

The love we share comes from God, not from us. From the Christian perspective, we are the signs of God's love, but we are not the source. An evangelist, therefore, has a duty to help people establish their own relationship with Jesus Christ. It is one thing to offer Christ's love to them; it is another to help them find faith in God themselves.

One must reject agendas and tactics. Traditionally, evangelists have used both fear and promise to bring people to faith. When my daughter was eight years old, for example, we sent her to a neighborhood church for a Vacation Bible School. What seemed like a fun way to teach her more about Jesus turned out to be an emotionally traumatic experience. Apparently willing to gain converts at any cost, they showed the children a movie about the Book of Revelation and the end of the world! Using fear to coerce children is spiritually and emotionally abusive. It is no less appropriate for adults, yet it is a technique well-established in Christian circles.

Whether or not one fears death, hell or some veiled description of the wrath of God, faith is never arrived at through fear. This is because the God presented through such evangelism is a God of which to be afraid, not the God of Jesus. "Fear of the Lord" is referred to in the Bible, but Paul's letter to the Romans offers the insight that we need not be afraid of God because of Jesus. God loves us unconditionally: "But God proves his love for us in that while we still were sinners, Christ died for us. Much more surely then, now that we have been justified by his blood, will we be saved through him from the wrath of God." (Romans 5:8-9)

Nor can faith be arrived at through the promise of a reward. While there are many-fold blessings received through faith in Christ, if one believes only to serve one's material or spiritual ends, one is simply striking a bargain. To place ultimate concern for self in the hands of God is the mark of faith, and remains the challenge of our lives as we grow in the grace and power of Christ's spirit.

The preoccupation about going to heaven within the Christian community (at the exclusion of others) reveals its persuasive power to win souls. Heaven is, indeed, an expectation because of God's love for us, but when it is used as the carrot to evoke faith, the point of faith is missed. Reconciliation with God through Jesus Christ is what it means to be in heaven. It begins in this life, and is a joy which surpasses understanding. Yet, faith is the way of the cross: suffering, persecution, and sacrifice for the benefit of others. It is the joy of servanthood.

A personal relationship with Jesus does not increase our status with God in comparison with other human beings. James and John were seeking such status as they conversed with Jesus on the road to Jerusalem, "Grant us to sit, one at your right hand and one at your left, in your glory." But Jesus said to them, "You do not know what you are asking." He went on to imply two things, that they would suffer as he would, and that it is not for us to make such decisions for God. The dialogue ended with his words, "The Son of Man came not to be served but to serve, and to give his life a ransom for many." (Mark 10:35-45)

If fear and reward are not sound tools for evangelism, then what is? In a word, it is witnessing. If you yourself are being transformed in Christ's love, there will be a "fragrance" which causes others to be drawn to the love within you. Then it is simply a matter of introducing them to Jesus Christ as your friend and theirs.

The Holy Spirit will give you the words to say when you speak from a loving heart.

EVANGELISM

Is Jesus the only way to salvation?

A conversation was overheard at the employees' water fountain between a born-again Christian and a Roman Catholic. While waiting for the Roman Catholic to pour from the fountain, the born-again said, "Did you know that Mother Theresa is not going to heaven." After pausing for a moment, shocked and hurt by the insult, the Roman Catholic responded, "Oh really? I don't think that bothers her very much." This exchange actually happened, and is typical of attitudes which can creep into our faith perspectives.

I suppose we've all had at least one instance where someone expressed their concern for our salvation. It may have been such a born-again friend or the knock on our door from a traveling missionary.

As a Christian, I trust in Jesus Christ as the means of salvation. Christian faith reveals a God who became incarnate as a human being and gave his life for the salvation of the whole world. There are many ways to describe how this happened in Jesus.

Perhaps most simply put, it is that we are loved so much that God came to tell us that anything we might do to separate ourselves from our creator is forgiven. We are invited to receive this grace and to live it in our own lives so that it becomes real for us and for others.

There is only one way to be saved, and that is to accept salvation as a gift. This is the point of Jesus' ministry. There are those who do not know Jesus personally, yet do know the reality of such salvation.

On the other hand, there are those who know Jesus who miss the point of his message, those who place conditions upon the unconditional love of God. It seems to me that if we understand Jesus not simply as revealed through our own historical traditions, but as the Lord of all life, then we must be open to his working in ways beyond our own experiences. We can do this while joyfully sharing our own knowledge of him.

There are those who say that only fellow Christians are brothers and sisters. This misses the mark of Christian faith. Through the eyes of Jesus, all human beings are children of God, whether they are aware of it or not.

The work of Christians is to help those unaware know that they are loved children of God. It is their inheritance from God. Sharing the good news is not a matter of warning someone that they are not saved. Rather, it is a matter of helping them appropriate the reality that they are saved.

We are all children of God. Some of us just don't know it yet. The urgency of evangelism is not that we are concerned about people's welfare ultimately (we trust that to God's mercy); it is that we are called to bring the love of God into this world through lives which are healed, renewed and empowered by God.

For the faithful to think that they are on the "inside" and others are on the "outside" is to fall into the arrogance of collective self-righteousness. Jesus confronted this attitude strongly and constantly both in his teaching and his actions. Humility and respect for the dignity of all of God's creation is the appropriate disposition for people of faith. Jesus modeled this in his relationships.

Whether born-again, Roman Catholic, mainline Church or orthodox, let us be worthy of his calling if we truly believe he is "The way, the truth, and the life."

I don't like to treat door-to-door evangelists rudely, but when I give them the slightest encouragement they come even more frequently. What should I do?

It is important to stop and think about what is really going on. While you attempt to be friendly and enter into meaningful conversation, they are there with an agenda to convert you to their way of thinking.

While you may enjoy the dialogue for awhile, ultimately you will either have to give in to the ever-tightening net of their argument or ask them to leave. If you're not comfortable with either of those options, then you might as well not encourage them in the first place and politely ask them not to visit you again.

They will say that they care about you, and are concerned for your salvation. Call me a cynic, but anyone who feels that you must belong to their group in order to be right with God cannot at the same time say they care about you. If they really cared, they would know how much God loves you and wants you to know that you don't have to join a particular sect in order to be loved. This kind of evangelism is an insult to you and is a distortion of Christ's love.

Evangelism is integral to Christian faith. We are called to proclaim the unconditional love of God which we have learned through the life, death, and resurrection of Jesus as God incarnate. When we deny the validity of other faith traditions, however, we have made an idol out of our own, even if it is in the name of Jesus Christ.

According to Mark 6:7, Jesus sent the disciples out two by two. They were not prepared to preach the good news. They had not yet experienced the crucifixion. They were consumed unambiguously by their ambitious, nationalistic goals, while still in the process of understanding Jesus' identity. By the time the Gospel was written, Christians would read into their mission an endeavor not unlike St. Paul's. But the twelve had no idea what the good news meant for them or for the homes they would visit.

Jesus' goal for the disciples when he sent them out was not for them to teach, but to learn. In fact, the story is told in the context of Jesus teaching the people. He gave them authority over evil spirits, ordered them to take nothing for their own material needs, and instructed them to stay only where they were welcomed. The result of their journey is that they drove out many evil spirits and healed many people by anointing them with oil. The message of their preaching was that people should turn away from their sins, the same message preached by John the Baptist.

What did Jesus want the disciples to learn? To trust him. His authority would have to be unquestioned in their minds because he would soon be teaching them the true meaning of the Gospel, loving service to all people, even sinners and enemies. They would later need to remember the power of God working through them to heal in order to get beyond what would become profound disappointment and fear when Jesus was crucified. On their first journey without Jesus, he taught them that oneness with God is not a matter of belonging to a spiritual club, but available to all through trust.

What is fundamentally wrong with the kind of evangelism expressed through most door-to-door efforts is that it dishonors the resident. When Jesus asked to be invited into Zaccheus' home, he was simply glad to spend some time with him. Zaccheus was a sinner in the eyes of his community, yet Jesus didn't require Zaccheus to accept a doctrine, join his band of followers, or even to repent. He accepted him and loved him as he was. Unconditional acceptance dramatically changed Zaccheus' behavior, but none of that was required for Jesus to honor him.

Evangelists would be true to Christ by honoring others rather than trying to change them. The greatest of life's treasures lies in receiving and offering such love. Evangelism with strings attached is not evangelism at all.

> *My sister-in-law is an avowed atheist and I am a practicing Christian. Every time we get together she manages to get in one or two negative remarks about how hypocritical and stupid Christians are. To keep peace I never respond or argue, though I find her comments hurtful. I know she'll never change her views, yet I think I should stand up for what I believe. She does! What do you suggest I do?*

Your question has both a personal and a theoretical aspect to it. On the one hand, your sister-in-law is hurting your feelings, and on the other she is stating an opinion which may have nothing to do with you personally.

Your sister-in-law may be trying to send you a personal message by speaking negatively about Christians in general. Since she brings it up every time you are together, I suspect this is the case.

The issue is one of respect for you and your beliefs, not Christianity itself. It is also possible that she is attracted to what you have but unwilling to admit it. She is obviously trying to engage you on the subject and you are avoiding it. It is important for the quality of your relationship and for your own spiritual growth to address these things with her.

First, try to clarify what is going on. You might begin along these lines: "It is certainly true that Christians, like everyone else, can be hypocritical and stupid, but you bring it up so often that I feel you may be trying to give me a message. In thinking about this I've considered whether you are trying to change my beliefs, or whether you accept me as I am. I've even wondered if you were baiting me to defend my faith as though you wanted to hear more about it through me. Sometimes I've felt hurt, and I realize it's largely because I don't know why you say these things. Can you clarify this for me?"

Here's another possible tack: "You've mentioned the hypocrisy and stupidity of Christians many times to me. I've seen these things, too. Christians, after all, are human beings. I feel that way myself sometimes. Would you share with me some of the experiences you've had which make you feel so strongly about it?" Then you might share with her some of your own experiences which allow you to value your Christian faith in the midst of human failings.

Hopefully, one of these approaches will evoke an honest sharing and increase the level of trust and communication between you. Most probably, however, she will not claim any ulterior motive and you can let it stand there. I can assure you she will not bring it up again because you have called her on this little game she is playing. If she does bring it up again, you are giving her permission to be more direct with you.

Beyond the personal level, there is the question of how to share your faith in loving ways. This is the task of evangelism. Every Christian is called to this ministry from "ordination" at baptism.

Evangelism at its best is sharing your story while honoring and respecting the dignity and beliefs of others. You can only be a witness to what you know to be true, and when you tell your own Good News, you are fulfilling your charge to pass on to others what you have received.

It is not your job to convert anyone. That is God's work. Your job is to speak of what you know in a loving way. The task of each Christian is not to convince others of doctrinal truths, but to be true to the love of Jesus Christ in word and deed. Our actions speak louder than anything we can say. If we humbly concentrate on the quality of our own relationship with God and our neighbor, we will be speaking volumes.

Please realize that there is more to evangelism than not hurting anyone. Christians are called to be proactive. God's transforming love takes the initiative and invites a response. Its beneficiary is often taken aback, surprised by its remarkable character in contrast with normal ways of the world.

Evangelism is more than doing what is right; it is doing what is exceedingly good. It is entering into a new world which transforms the status quo, the world of unconditional love. The biblical stories, therefore, are teeming with examples of the unbounded joy and transforming generosity of God, especially in the life of Jesus.

The proactive nature of Christian life does not imply being pedantic or didactic. On the contrary, it is servanthood which seeks to express the value which God holds toward every human being.

You can share you faith with your sister-in-law by taking the initiative. You honor her by seeking to clarify her intent and inviting her into dialogue. It is a loving act for you to share your own experience with her because by doing so you are trusting her. If she responds in hurtful ways, try to remember that the essence of your self-esteem comes not from her but from God.

By the way, the word "martyr" means witness. To humbly witness for God always requires overcoming our fears.

Something in my church is worrying me. My pastor does not believe in helping the members of our church if they are unable to tithe. I asked if we could help a family in need, and he said he hoped they don't become a charity case. I don't think my pastor is reading James 5:14-16. What should I do?

Keep up the good work. We pastors can sometimes become cynical with the many requests for help that come our way. It is appropriate for people to confront their pastors when they see them acting in ways which may be inconsistent with the message they speak from the pulpit.

Jesus himself, on at least one occasion, was confronted with such inconsistency. There is a story in the Gospel of Mark where

Jesus is enlightened by another person, remarkable not only because of the content but also because the story was preserved. It does not portray Jesus as the sanitized epitome of human perfection which we like to see.

As is so often the case in the Bible, the means of revelation is a woman. She also was not Hebrew. In other words, she should not have been the source of growth for anyone, let alone Jesus, according to conventional wisdom, but she was. Jesus was reminded of his true identity because of her response to him.

The story begins at Mark 7:24. The woman begged Jesus to cast a demon out of her daughter. Jesus said to her, "Let the children be fed first, for it is not fair to take the children's food and throw it to the dogs." But she answered him, "Sir, even the dogs under the table eat the children's crumbs." Then Jesus said to her, "For saying that, you may go — the demon has left your daughter."

In his humanity, Jesus appears in this instance to be subject to the prejudice of his people toward Gentiles. Perhaps he was tired of the many requests for help, thinking he had gotten away for awhile by going to a Gentile area. In any case, her humility and her faith - her wisdom - jarred him back into the truth of his calling.

There are, of course, other ways of interpreting this passage. Some would soften it and explain away the possibility that Jesus would be subject to the prejudices of his people or the weaknesses of the flesh. I prefer the interpretation that in his humanity, Jesus responded to her uncharacteristically. That reveals a God who loves us enough to become fully human. I find it comforting. It makes my faith stronger.

I also believe that it teaches us that it is out of such less-than-ideal circumstances that truth is revealed. Had Jesus not been rudely short with her, he may not have become aware of his prejudice. The issue for us is whether we, like Jesus, are humble enough to learn from such imperfect moments in our lives. The power of the story is not in the woman's humility, but in Jesus'.

There is another point which needs to be made in response to your question. Remember, you only know a piece of the story. You are right to express you concern to your pastor and to do yourself what you feel may be helpful. The pastor most likely has more information than you do, however.

His reluctance to help may be because he knows that a hand-out at this time would not be best for this family. He may know they have the ability to help themselves. He may feel the church has helped them to their detriment in the past.

Whatever the reason, there are times when we need to trust the wisdom of our pastor because of the confidential information which only the pastor knows. This possibility must always be weighed. But never shy away from speaking your heart. From what little you've told me, I know the Lord will use you powerfully.

On Ash Wednesday I find the imposition of ashes to be very meaningful, but I am uncomfortable walking around all day with ashes on my forehead. Jesus said not to display publicly our piety, but I'm not really comfortable removing the ashes, either. What do you recommend?

The Imposition of Ashes gives Ash Wednesday its name, of course, and is an ancient Christian ceremony marking the beginning of Lent. Usually the words from Genesis, "Remember that you are dust, and to dust you shall return" are recited as the priest makes the sign of the cross with ashes upon the forehead.

Because Lent is the season in which we focus upon repenting our sins to God, the ashes say, "Without God's forgiveness, our life ends in ashes."

I, like you, find the ashes to be a powerful symbol. For me, it is a kind of a wake-up call. Life is a gift, and so is eternal life. Just as God gave us biological life, God can be trusted to fill us with eternal life, but in the latter, we have a choice in the matter. The ashes are a wake-up call to turn away from the false gods of the world and give our lives to the one true God who is our creator.

With that brief background for readers who may not be familiar with this tradition, what do we do about the ashes on our forehead? When we read Matthew 6 and the surrounding material in Jesus' "Sermon on the Mount," it is clear that he is not providing rules to follow, but rather asking his audience to take a look at their motives. If one's motive is to prove how pious one is, then that goal may be accomplished, but nothing more is gained. As Jesus says, "They have their reward."

Notice that in the midst of Jesus' teaching about hypocrisy, he also teaches the audience how to pray. This has become known as "The Lord's Prayer." Since he uses the prayer in this context, he is saying, "If you want to impress others, that's one thing, but if you want to impress God, then honor God, humbly seek God's will, trust God, and treat others the way God treats you." That's what The Lord's Prayer says, in so many words.

So I ask you to examine your motives. I would suggest that if you want people to know that you have been to church and are a religious person, then wash your face quickly! But if you want to honor God with every word and action, seek God's will in every decision, trust God for the consequences when you have tried to follow the way of God's love, and be a means of God's grace to others, then, by all means, leave the ashes on.

There is no reason to be shy about witnessing to your faith as long as your actions are compatible with the symbols you present. Many wear crosses and some members of the clergy wear special clothing. These can be important reminders that life is more than our worldly pursuits. They can stimulate conversation, and at the very least be a subtle statement of whence your love comes. Ashes are almost sure to spark a reaction.

Here's an idea for what to say when someone says, "Hey, did you know you have a smudge on your forehead?"

"Yes, I know. Thank you. It's Ash Wednesday, the beginning of Lent." Then, let the other person carry the conversation. It may end there, or it may be the beginning of an opportunity for you to share your belief that without God's forgiveness, your life would be ashes.

FAMILY AND FRIENDS

I was at a wedding recently where the minister said that the role of the wife is to submit to the spiritual leadership of the husband, and that the role of the husband is to love his wife. My husband loves me, but never goes to church or prays. How can I get him to accept his God-given responsibility?

The teaching of the minister at the wedding is a common interpretation of Ephesians 5:21-33. The passage applies the love of Jesus Christ to marital relationships at the time of the early church. While the instruction seems unambiguous, the historical situation must be taken into account.

Ephesians was written in a culture where men and women did not have equal status. The material and spiritual inheritance of women was derived from the men to whom they were born or married. Without a man, a woman had no status at all, and in marriage was more like property than a partner. In our time and place, the passage must be interpreted differently.

The intent of the passage is to teach us to work within the "givens" of our situation in order to offer our uniqueness to one another and to grow in the love of Christ. While marriage then was a hierarchical structure with men spiritually above women, spouses in our culture are viewed as equal partners in God's plan of salvation and growth. (This is still resisted, of course, in some traditional circles.)

The understanding of the relationship between men and women evolves as God leads humanity forward in the unfolding

145

development of human wholeness. The spirit of the passage cited above is in the first verse, "Be subject to one another out of reverence for Christ." Your task, therefore, is not to figure out how to get your husband to accept his God-given responsibility. He must do that for himself.

Your task is to become yourself more fully as a child of God. By focusing upon your own spiritual journey into wholeness, you can best love others. If your husband does not begin to take responsibility for his own spiritual growth, your self-discovery and discovery of God's loving presence within you will still reap rewards and bear fruit in your life.

As you relate to your husband, it is important to keep in mind this idea that each of us is called to make his own spiritual journey. One way of describing this journey might be that it is a life of "humble assertiveness." That means that we are practicing the way of becoming more true to God's call to us. Like the acorn which gradually becomes the great oak, we are at our best when we build our lives in communion with the potential which is within us.

This is never a straight and sure path, but a complex one of continuous choices between the forward movement of alignment with God (life) and the backward movement of misalignment (death). We don't always make life-offering choices. The way forward is often only clear in retrospect. But God's grace is always with us to pick us up and utilize our mistakes to make us ever more beautiful and helpful in the co-creation process.

Humble assertiveness means that we will not be put down. It is our duty to realize our own gifts and respond outwardly to the unique persons which God has created us to be and become. We often try to fulfill the expectations of loved ones rather than God's. We try to fit the roles which society imposes upon us, even when we don't feel they are appropriate for us. Spiritual maturity, however, empowers us to assert ourselves lovingly.

When we have been put down by others, be they parents, faith communities or spouse, there is bound to be anger. We want to strike back. Sometimes we direct such anger at ourselves because we have let this happen.

The solution to this sense of loss and impairment is to remember the ways God has loved us, to allow ourselves to soak up the love that God pours out to us, and to begin to respond with our lives to that love that is within us. This is what is meant by being subject to Christ. It is the motivation to become more fully who we are.

So let God work on your husband and claim your own inheritance in relationship with God. I suspect he will be attracted to the light and lightness which is the sign of your increasing wholeness, and want it for himself. Hopefully, he will not be threatened by it. In any case, you are choosing the path of life.

I want my children to have a spiritual "base." Besides sending them to Sunday School, what other specific things might parents do to engender this quality?

The most important thing parents can do for the spiritual foundation of their children is to be alive spiritually themselves. The old saying is true, "Faith is caught, not taught." Children are "infected," for better or worse, with what their parents have. When parents are authentic in their own faith, children will find their lives patterned around the values, the nourishment and the lessons learned from the traditions of their faith family.

Many parents attend a church because of the children. For them, spiritual awareness and growth is a childhood thing which they have outgrown themselves. Without realizing it, they have placed faith in God in the same relevance as Santa Claus and the Easter Bunny. Faith becomes a children's myth serving a developmental need at best, but it is not real. While it is hoped that a lasting relationship with God may quicken within a child whose parents own faith lacks vitality, it is often the case that such an early "inoculation" prevents the true experience of faith from ever taking hold.

If faith is vital to parents, it will most likely be vital to their children. We cannot be sure that our children will inherit faith from us, but we can be sure that they will perceive intuitively at very young ages any presence of hypocrisy, insincerity or lack of enthusiasm.

I suggest the following exercise: Ask yourself how important your faith truly is. Where does faith rank with other aspects of your life - family, self-fulfillment, career, recreation, whatever. This is not a test. There is no pass or fail, no right answers. Be honest. For the sake of simplification, let's say there are three possible answers: Most important, somewhat important and not important.

If you answered "most important," then ask yourself if you have prioritized your life in such a way that the importance of faith is expressed in your daily life. Are you providing for yourself opportunities to learn and grow in faith? Do you set time aside for personal devotions and worship with your fellow believers? Have you developed the tools which allow you to be open to the presence of God, and do you have a sense of unfolding spiritual maturity?

Ask yourself if your children could say from their experience that God is the most important part of your life.

If you answered "somewhat important," ask yourself why God is not more important to you. Your answer implies that you believe God exists. There must be reasons why other aspects of life are more important. Your reflections will help you build a theology and then you can decide if you are happy with it. For example, it may be "God exists, but is too busy to have a personal relationship with me." Or, "God exists, but I am unable to know God." Articulate your thoughts about God and share these with your children in age-appropriate ways. Warning: If you do this, you will probably find your faith growing because you are giving it some attention.

If you answered "not important," your answer may say you don't hold a basic belief in God. Again, ask why. Many have been affected or even abused by self-righteous, judgmental believers. Others have simply never heard the love of God expressed in their "language."

But there doesn't have to be a reason. You have the right to your beliefs, and you owe your children the values you hold.

The best way to give a spiritual base to your child is to be standing on one yourself!

FAMILY and FRIENDS

*My children are 12 and 14
and do not want to go to church, even though we have
been regular attendees as a family all of their lives.
What advice do you have to get them to church?*

Children usually begin to resist going to church with the family in their pre-adolescent years, and certainly by the time they are full-blown teen-agers. As parents, we must face the fact that our teens usually don't want to be seen anywhere with us, even though they may be perfectly comfortable with the parents of their peers or other adults.

Don't feel that you've failed. Resist the temptation to be offended personally. Such a universally experienced phenomenon must have a purpose. Children need to begin to formulate their own ideas and make their own choices, as frightening as that process may be for us. Nonetheless, here are some tips for parents.

Don't attend church for your children, but for yourselves. It is not unusual for parents to begin to attend a church when their children are young, raise them as regular churchgoers for as long as possible, getting involved themselves as parents, but then "retiring" from the church when the children are raised or will no longer go. Their motivation is something like, "We want to give the children a good spiritual foundation."

In reality, this thinking gives no foundation at all. It simply conveys the idea that a religious community is valuable for children, not for adults. Is it any wonder that when the children begin to become adults they lose interest?

Parents who become involved in their church communities because they seek spiritual fullness for themselves model for their children the importance of church for adults. Such parents are probably more obvious in living their faith at home as well, thus incorporating the values of faith into their children's daily lives and extending the time they will value it as young teens.

When parents continue to grow in their own faith as individuals and as couples, children intuitively learn that they have something to look forward to spiritually when they reach adulthood. Be completely honest. Don't pretend to value church for yourself. Doing so will almost guarantee that your children will not have a meaningful faith as adults.

Invest in your church's youth program, and expect the leadership to do so. Children should never be forced to go to church when they reach the age of making many of their own choices. Good children's programs will attract them.

Yes, I know the old saw that we wouldn't let them choose whether or not to go to school, so why church? But church is different. You see, faith is a choice we make, and church should be one of the choices children make when they begin making some of their own decisions.

Therefore, your church needs to be a place they will choose to be, not where they are forced to go. If the climate is aimed only at adults, kids will be bored. Do all that you can to create the kind of climate that your children will not be able to resist while you continue to aid them in the maturation of their faith.

Go with the flow. Sometimes our kids need to be somewhere where we are not. Be thankful if they want to go with their friends to a different church. Churches tend to go in cycles as to where the hottest youth ministry is at any given time. This is not only because of the ebb and flow of church priorities and politics, but also the fluctuating demographics of the area and the need for young people to collect where their peers are.

Keep good communication going about their experiences. Sincerely seek to learn from them about the differences and commonalities of their experience with what your family church teaches. Above all, affirm them in their ability to think for themselves, even though you know they will make mistakes.

Be patient. The formation of a meaningful spiritual life includes periods of dryness, sometimes for years, and one of these appropriately occurs during teen and young adult years. Spirituality may seem to take a back seat to sexuality, career pursuits and financial success, but after all, don't we need to learn first-hand about the false gods before we can really trust the true One?

*I have tried everything to get
my husband to stop drinking. He is a different person
when he gets drunk, becoming abusive and embarrass-
ing to me and our children. I know Alcoholics Anony-
mous is helpful, but how do I get him to go?*

Y ou are describing a family which is under the influence of alcohol, and I commend you for asking for help. Too many people
remain in feelings of despair and powerlessness when there is lots
of help around. I don't want to imply, however, that the path toward healing and wholeness is an easy one.

One of the difficult aspects of coping with alcoholism is the
matter of denial. The person who abuses alcohol is usually the last
to admit that he or she is addicted, and other family members who
suffer the consequences are reluctant to seek treatment as well.
Overcoming denial is the first step, and it sounds as though you
have done this.

I suggest as a next step to do your best to get out from under
the power of alcohol yourself. Without realizing it, you have organized your life around alcohol as much as your husband has. You
probably try to avoid certain situations, protect the children, hide
the bottle, etc.

In order to "get sober" yourself, you will need to learn how to
act from within yourself rather than to react to your husband's
drinking problem.

The best way I know to do that is to seek the information and
support that is available to you from a self-help group known as
Alanon. Alanon supports family members of alcoholics who recognize that they have become part of the illness of alcoholism themselves, and help one another to form healthier patterns of thought
and living.

If one or both of your parents were alcoholics, a group called
Adult Children of Alcoholics might be appropriate. These groups
are in the telephone directory and meet regularly at a variety of
times in every community.

Don't neglect the children. Regardless of their age, they are
profoundly affected by alcoholism and the earlier you start establishing healthier patterns for yourself, the healthier they will be

emotionally. If they are teen-agers, there is AlaTeen.

If attending a group would be intimidating for you right now, you can read the wealth of literature available in book stores, usually under the heading of co-dependence. I also encourage you to talk to your pastor or a professional counselor, most of whom are well-versed these days in recovery issues.

The essence of what you will learn to do is to live successfully regardless of what your husband chooses to do. Though this won't solve all of your problems, of course, this will be liberating for you. You will begin to bring more order and healthy communication into your family, modeling these qualities for your children. You will find that you have the power to lead a peaceful, centered life.

It is truly a lifetime process. That's why you hear people say, even after years of sobriety that they are alcoholics. They are recovering alcoholics, but they are alcoholics.

The same is true for families of alcoholics. They are recovering co-dependents, learning and relearning how to live in healthy patterns throughout their lives.

Once you are on your road to recovery, you can then be of help to your husband. You will have the tools and support to truly help, rather than contributing to the sickness because you are enmeshed in it.

There is a basic principle of the spiritual life which needs to be emphasized: Every experience of suffering brings with it an opportunity to awaken our relationship with God. The desperation you express in your question is leading you to new awareness and growth within yourself which you could not have obtained had you not been driven into action by frustration.

By the grace of God, the pain you are experiencing can be transformed into new life for you. Admitting your powerlessness and trusting in God is an important first step.

Would you please address the O.J. Simpson matter?

The only point of my adding to the great wealth of commentary on this murder is to explore what I have not seen discussed, the spiritual issues.

If this murder was the crazed act of a jealous and possessive man, as the prosecution argues (and he has not been convicted), then he was a man whose ultimate meaning in life was being threatened.

The core spiritual issue in abuse cases is idolatry. Idolatry is when we give our primary loyalty to or receive our primary identity from, something other than God. In this case, it was another person.

When ultimate meaning is threatened, we will do almost anything to control events or to numb the pain, even murder or suicide. It is not unusual for people who seem to have everything going for them to act in such an irrational way - to put it all at risk - because they cannot tolerate the idea that someone else might take away what gives their life ultimate meaning. It is no surprise that people kill for drugs, or even for money, and it should not surprise us that we can become so obsessed that we kill what we want but cannot have.

Abusive men are afraid of losing the object of their love. This causes them to be very controlling, and their domineering ways have the effect, of course, of bringing about exactly what they fear. This drives them to control more, and the vicious craziness escalates with each successive incident. In time, all perspective is lost.

This syndrome can occur with women toward men, but is more common in men because of the tendency toward dominance which men seem to possess and the long tradition of patriarchy which legitimizes the "ownership" of women. (Thankfully, society and our churches are becoming more aware of this subtle influence upon our behavior and attitudes.)

The syndrome can also occur between parents and children. A parent may not go so far as to kill a child, but we certainly can go to extremes far beyond what is healthy for our children in our efforts to control them.

I have known parents who have had a very painful and difficult adjustment to their children leaving home because they have invested their ultimate meaning in keeping their children dependent upon them. Although it seems crazy to us, we are not surprised to hear stories of people who commit suicide in the face of other losses, be it money, youth, career, or a loved one.

The common ingredient in all of the above is that people have placed ultimate trust in that which is ultimately not trustworthy. Then they take senseless measures to try to make the "other" into that which it cannot be. Failing that, they may be driven to destroy it or themselves.

The crucifixion of Jesus might be seen in the light of this tendency on the part of humanity to destroy what fails our need for a worldly savior. Our passion for tangible gods is insatiable. And while we pursue these false gods (idols), we are killing the possibility of a relationship with the one God who can give our lives true value and purpose, what the Bible calls "eternal life."

It is this misplaced trust which also makes it very difficult for women to end abusive relationships when they realize they are in one. A woman who has a healthy self-esteem would probably not be attracted to an abusive man, and if she is deceived until she is committed to such a man, she will have the inner strength to end it before it gets to the point of no return.

Tragically, an abusive man seems to know when a woman does not have such strength, and targets her. Of course, he is often not aware himself of what is happening. At whatever stage of this unhealthy dynamic, the road to healing and recovery begins with an understanding that the problem is a spiritual one with psychological symptoms. It is one of misplaced trust and ultimate dependence upon a false god.

One response we can all make to the "O.J. Simpson matter" is to try to be healthier spiritually. If our ultimate meaning in life does not come from God, then we are on dangerous ground. At the very least, we are at risk of losing ultimate meaning because the tangible things of life are also transitory.

In the worst case scenario, we may become so fearful of losing our ultimate love that we become irrational in our efforts to control it in order to maintain our happiness.

If God is the source of ultimate meaning, then the rest of our lives can be kept in an appropriate perspective. The creatures of God are given to be enjoyed and nurtured, and do indeed, give our lives great meaning. A vital and intentional relationship with God will allow us to enjoy the blessings of God without becoming obsessed by them.

*I am concerned about the
materialism of Christmas and Easter. I want my children to appreciate the true meaning of these holy days,
but it's hard to get their minds off of Santa Claus and
toys, or at Easter, the EasterBunny and baskets of candy.
What do you recommend?*

The commercial popularity of Christmas and Easter is both a
blessing and a curse to those for whom these days are observances of the saving actions of God.

Your problem is shared not only by Christians, but also by
Jewish families and others who try to focus on the meaning of their
holy days while immersed in a culture determined to secularize and
exploit them.

So what do we as people of faith do? Why not go with the
flow? Secular holiday customs can communicate the Godly message we want our children to receive.

This is what Christians have done over history. They have
not isolated themselves from the secular world, but have sanctified
it. The perspective was that these secular celebrations contain the
goodness of God's love for humanity, but like blurred pictures, need
to be brought into focus to reflect God's unconditional love contained
in the experience of Jesus Christ.

Jesus himself used everyday life experiences to teach about
the Kingdom of God. St. Paul used the devotions of the Greeks to
the Unknown God to proclaim Jesus.

In the early Fourth Century, Christians began to celebrate
the birth of Jesus adopting the date of the secular observances of
the "Birth of the Sun," the Winter Solstice, when the days began to
be longer again.

Likewise, Easter replaced an ancient pagan festival of spring.
According to the Venerable Bede, 8th century "Father of English
History," the word itself comes from an Anglo-Saxon spring goddess, "Eoster." And, of course, the Christian calendar itself is based
loosely upon the Jewish calendar of sacred feasts.

Since Easter is upon us, here are some ways you can teach
your children about the Good News of God's love using the very
symbols they enjoy so much.

First, the egg is an ancient sign of new life. Though it appears dead, the egg is very much alive, awaiting only the fullness of God's plan. This is the theology of Resurrection - the core of Christian faith.

Followers of Jesus began to experience his presence in new and powerful ways after his death. This continuing personal relationship with Jesus as a living and transforming presence, is the heart of Christian experience.

Teach your children that even when they don't feel that Jesus is with them, or when they are afraid, or when they have experienced a loss, that Jesus is indeed with them, and, like the egg, appearances are not all that they seem.

We color the Easter Egg to remind ourselves that something beautiful is being created on the inside of lifeless experiences. We need to trust God, act according to our faith, and wait for the fullness of God's time.

Second, the Easter bunny can be a kind of angel, who hides the eggs in places where we would not expect to find them. God invites us to walk into places we might not want to go on our own wisdom.

For example, to live a life of service to others is not the way to accumulate riches. Yet, the blessings for us when we do walk in faith surprise us by their overwhelming peace and joy.

The Way of the Cross is an inseparable part of the celebration of Easter. We find new life in discovering truths hidden in unlikely places, giving our lives in love to all people, even the unlovable.

Finally, the matter of candy at Easter. Sure, it's not good for us. But nothing says "celebration" to a child more than candy. It represents pure, unbounded joy.

When you give your children Easter Baskets this year, make sure they know that this is an expression of both your joy in them and God's love for them.

As your children mature as people of faith, they will have many challenges to translate their faith into the context of every day life. You can help them to think theologically by interpreting the holiday signs they cherish as expressions of God's grace.

Is there any connection be-
tween the Easter Bunny, Easter Eggs, and Christianity?

There is an ancient Christian relevance to the Easter Egg as a symbol of the Resurrection. Eggs appear to be lifeless, like white sepulchers, yet they contain the beginnings of new life. A basic Christian tenet, that true life is born from the least likely places, is thus derived from the humble egg.

Especially prominent in the Orthodox tradition of Christianity, Easter Eggs are ornately decorated and colored beautifully, usually red, to celebrate the grace of God which brings life from that which appears to be dead. Easter Eggs are signs of hope in the midst of hopelessness, a reminder that all things are possible with God.

The Easter Egg Hunt itself can be a parable of the Kingdom of God. Children feel excitement, anticipation, and joy. They urgently pursue the goal of finding the prize. They have an intuitive sense that waiting creates missed opportunities.

Christians have always made use of local and secular customs to teach the faith wherever the Gospel has spread. That's because they find the grace of God at work beyond the traditions of the Church. Thus, we can cooperate with the Easter Bunny in teaching our faith to children. Coloring eggs with children can be a great opportunity to discuss the meaning of Christian faith and provide spiritual tools for them to call upon when they experience the trials we all face in life.

As children hunt for eggs, they have no idea where the eggs are, but they know they are there. It would be unthinkable to invite a child on a hunt where no eggs have been hidden, unthinkable because trust is built into the tradition. It is not only that children will find eggs, but that every child will find eggs. The adults and older children hide the eggs in places not too difficult to find, and in so doing teach children that God can be trusted to be found if one searches.

Children usually spot the eggs because they see an object with a color which is out of context with its surroundings. While the world teaches us to build a context for our lives which will guarantee success, faith teaches that true life comes from faith's response

157

when our plans go sour. Preparations always fail us eventually. The Easter Bunny is the trickster who turns our plans up-side-down and makes life's true blessings a little harder to find. We are challenged through life's struggles to discover a more meaningful and enduring way of living. Have you ever noticed in children's stories how rabbits are usually portrayed as tricksters, as in Brer Rabbit, Bugs Bunny, and the Mad Hatter?

Bunnies and eggs also tell us that God uses the ordinary stuff of our lives to communicate Grace. On Easter Sunday, millions of people take ordinary eggs and make them tokens of love and lessons in life. They proclaim the message that children are important and belong to a community who loves them. Eggs are wonderful food for growing bodies. At Easter, they feed the soul as well.

There is a final thought about God and Easter Eggs I want to share with you. The biblical message is not that we are searching for God, but that God is searching for us. The picture of the shepherd looking for lost sheep comes to mind, for example. Imagine God, then, as the child searching for the egg. You are the egg, in the world but not of the world, part of nature, yet decorated gloriously in God's image. The false self causes us to hide from God, as Adam and Eve did in the Garden of Eden. If we hide, we think we can stay in control. While we hear God calling, we are afraid to answer. We don't let our glory show too much for fear that God will find our hiding place.

Perhaps Easter is about letting God find our hiding places.

*Should a Christian partici-
pate in Halloween? As a school teacher and a parent, I
worry about all the fascination with evil and the occult
which is at the core of Halloween observances.*

Halloween literally means "All Hallows Eve," the eve of All Saints Day on the Christian calendar. It is difficult to discern between ancient Christian ideas and secular influences, but deep within the mists of Halloween's traditions lies the basic question: "How do we deal with evil in the world?"

The answer is that we respond the way Jesus and the saints did. As St. Paul said, "Do not be overcome by evil, but overcome evil with good."

Halloween was second only to Christmas in my childhood. I liked dressing up and pretending to be more powerful than I really was, going around extorting treats from adults by scaring them. Of course, the adults were in on the game and weren't frightened. One particular neighbor made wonderful cookies. To this day I can see her kind face as she feigned fear and then lovingly brought out the tray filled with the homemade treats. Sadly, we can't give homemade treats anymore.

Knowingly or not, she was teaching us about Jesus' response to evil. It exists, but because of the love of God, evil has no ultimate power over us. We need not be afraid. We are free to respond to evil with love. Halloween can be the celebration of Christ's victory over evil, and Christians can use Halloween to teach this important lesson to their children.

In my childhood ways I tried to do evil to my neighbors by scaring them to death, but they responded to me with kindness.

On the eve of All Saints' Day we remember not to live in fear and isolation from the world with all of its evils, but to love one's neighbor, even enemies, holding compassion for those who are hurting and angry, and trusting God through our ministry to help meet the world's needs.

There is another lesson in Halloween. Children can begin to learn that our outside is not necessarily what we feel on the inside. Help your children to begin to understand the importance of listening to themselves and of trying to live with integrity.

The simple act of putting on a costume can become a lesson in the concept of "putting on Christ." It's a matter of knowing that we are loved for who we are and living in ways that are true to our own calling while respectful of others. As children grow, they may wish to dress up as a saint rather than a goblin. They begin to learn that it's more fun to do good than to do evil.

Like it or not, we're stuck with Halloween. I suggest we seize the opportunity to grow in our faith while we live in the midst of an imperfect world. I think it's healthy for children to act our their fascination with frightening things in the context of a nurturing community. It keeps evil in perspective, not giving it too much power. It's also good for us as parents and teachers to learn to use such occasions of life as tools to help our children love God, themselves, and others.

> *Christmas has been taken over by the marketplace. What do you think Christians can do to "take back" the true meaning of Christmas?*

I don't worry too much about the commercialization of Christmas. I figure we should be grateful for the opportunity to share our faith. Whenever the public in general finds value in a religious tradition, there is great opportunity for people of faith to build upon their interest. It's not a matter of competing with secular exploitation, but rather of focusing it as much as possible to reveal the inherent message.

Ironically, the celebration of Christmas actually began by Christians borrowing from the world around them. There were great pagan festivals around the date of the Winter Solstice, so in the Fourth Century the Church set the date for celebrating Christ's birth at that time. No one knows exactly when Jesus was born. The date was chosen both for its symbolism (of light coming into darkness) and to give Christians a way to witness to their Lord unsurpassed in joy by their pagan neighbors.

What fuels Christmas in society today is, of course, money. Gift giving means gift buying. It can also be good for spreading the Gospel, however. Here's some ideas on how to use the process of gift giving as food for the soul.

Christians are sacramental people. You are a means of God's grace. Christmas means that God became incarnate in the person of Jesus and continues to use the "stuff" of the world as a means of grace through those who know Jesus Christ as Lord and Savior. That means you.

When you purchase gifts, you have many opportunities to share the love of Christ in an otherwise stressful environment. Do you see the sales clerk as a child of God? Are you sensitive to his or her needs, or do you see him or her as your servant? Can you say a little prayer as you purchase something, asking God to use you as an instrument to transform a mere monetary exchange into a moment of grace? In hectic situations try to make personal connections with strangers. A tender moment of compassion can engender an oasis of refreshment in the midst of the stress of the season.

What about your Christmas tree? You've spent a lot of time, money and effort on it. Have you discussed with your loved ones the feelings it evokes in you? What values does the tree represent for you? How would you express those values in terms of your relationship with God? The tree is a glorious symbol of the joy of God's loving and constant presence in our lives. It can also represent the wonder of the Body of Christ, with all of its ornaments symbolizing the diverse members, working together as poignant witnesses of God's love.

As you open gifts, be reminded that you are the package which contains the greatest gift ever given to human kind, the gift of God's unconditional love in Jesus Christ. Your opening that gift is a lifetime process of growing into the fullness of Christ in your own life. Gift giving and receiving are more than expressions of our love for one another; they are also expressions of God's call to us to be transformed into the Body of Christ.

Don't worry about the secular world stealing Christmas. This time of year provides lots of common ground upon which to share the story of a God who loved the world so much that he came to make a home with us.

A man in my church owes me money. When I confront him he makes promises which are never kept. I've tried to be patient, but this really is coming between us. It has spoiled going to church for me because I feel so much anger toward him. What do you suggest?

Your situation is an extreme example of what occurs commonly in relationships with faith communities. Feelings of abuse can interfere with our ability to worship wholeheartedly. After all, worship is not intended to be disassociated from the quality of our relationships. Jesus said, "If you are about to offer your gift to God at the altar and there you remember that your brother or sister has something against you, leave your gift there at the front of the altar, go at once and make peace with your brother or sister, and then come back and offer your gift to God." Your friend is ignoring this teaching of Jesus at the risk of his own spiritual well-being.

The church is part of an imperfect world. The following course of action might be helpful to you and others who find themselves in similar circumstances. Begin to set your goal to focus on your own spiritual life despite the abuse of your friend. People do not always meet our expectations or keep their commitments. While standing up for our rights, we cannot always get what we deserve from others. It is their responsibility to deal with their issues just as it is ours to deal with ours. Let your actions be motivated by the love of God within you, not your feelings of betrayal.

You may eventually have to take this person through the court system to protect your rights. Meanwhile, however, you want to be careful not to create a tug of war that may contain higher stakes. The issue of the money owed to you, for example, soon becomes an issue of your integrity versus his, your generosity versus his need, etc. Offenders tend to make accusations in order to justify or cloud irresponsible behavior. You are subject to hurt even further and the cycle of abuse expands.

When you have spent some time doing your spiritual homework, you will be able to deal with your friend in the love of God. One sign of your readiness is that you will consider reconciliation with your friend more important than getting your money back.

Another sign is that you will define your friend by the wholeness of this person rather than by the single act of taking advantage of you. Finally, you will recognize that this is likely not an isolated incident, but an example of unhealthy behavior which has plagued the quality of this person's life for years.

Notice how you have already begun to experience healing from your own hurt. You have begun to clothe this situation in the love of God by placing restoration as a priority and justice in a larger context. You are not ready to act with less risk of magnifying, and therefore becoming part of, the problem.

Jesus gave us some advice for your situation. You will find it in Matthew 18:15-17. His words reflect the reality that justice is always part of love, but love is not always part of justice. Therefore, to proceed in the higher context of love, one does well to seek God's guidance within the spiritual community first.

When you have dealt with the person prayerfully and patiently, and payment has not been made, then consult with two or three wise people whom you trust as spiritual friends. They do not have to know the identity of the offending person in order to help. Bear in mind these "witnesses" are not people you garner to be on your side, but rather people whom you seek because they are able to be objective. If you still do not have a clear sense of God's direction, seek the counsel of your pastor. He or she will help you to become spiritually whole as I've described above, and will also provide the perspective derived from their wisdom and experience.

By now you will know how to proceed with your friend, recognizing that your efforts are more for him than yourself. Hopefully, you will receive your money back and your friendship will be restored. In any case, you will have gained far more in treasures in heaven that the treasure on earth you might have lost.

Is it ever OK to tell a "white
lie?" I live in a resort area, and friends from out of
town often want to come and visit. I want to be nice to
them, but I really don't want them to stay at my home.
I resort to telling a white lie, but feel guilty about it.

There is always a better course than to lie. In your situation, I
believe the love of Jesus requires more of us than simply putting out the welcome mat. Kindness is one of the fruits of the spirit
given to those who seek to love as Christ loves us. But there is a
difference between being nice and being kind. Kindness demands
honesty, open communication, and a desire to truly help another
person.

We tend to judge the quality of our actions by their outward
appearances rather than inward feelings and motives which lie
behind them. Jesus consistently asked people to be aware of what
is on the inside as being more important to God and to others than
what is on the outside. To be hospitable when we do not want to is
hurtful to our guests, and probably shows.

If we are nice to people but feel abused, or lie to them for fear
of not being nice, we are not kind. Being nice is often an easy way
to avoid confrontation and the expression of honest feelings. It
takes a toll, however, in the quality of the relationship because it
plants seeds of resentment and emotional distance. We may take
some consolation in the thought that we have done our "Christian
duty," but this is false martyrdom.

On the other hand, kindness takes courage. We are afraid
that we might lose the friend by being truthful, but we need to
overcome this fear in order to build a friendship of openness and
trust.

So, the primary consideration is this: How can I say with
concern for the other person what is also truthful about my feelings? In your situation, how might this sound? "Fred, I would love
to see you while you are in Resortville, but I've found that I don't
enjoy people's visits when they stay with me. How can we schedule
some time together while you're here."

This kind of approach will separate those friends who really
want to be with you from those who simply want to use you. It will

also help them to confront their own feelings. People who care about you will want you to be honest. They would not want you to feel imposed upon. If they are offended that you are not willing to put them up, they are not the kind of friends you want.

By being honest, you are being loving because you care enough to be truthful, and because you are not allowing someone to take advantage of you unknowingly (or knowingly). You are helping the other person to be more loving, too. Some people will realize the gift you are giving them, a higher quality of friendship with you than you currently have.

The love of God is not built upon "niceness." It is built upon honesty, respect for one another, and the desire to do what is truly helpful, even when it is difficult for the other person to accept it.

Is it ever okay to tell a "white lie?" There is a theological possibility for an affirmative answer. For example, one might think of a situation when it would be the lesser of two evils. My hope would be that we not resort to white lies, but instead do our best to be lovingly honest.

Recently while attempting to care for an older friend, I made a decision for her which she could have made and ended up hurting her deeply. I know now that I was wrong to do so, even though at the time I thought it was best. What can I do to reconcile this relationship?

We all make these kinds of mistakes. When people are the recipients of our care, whether our children, elderly parents, clients or anybody whom we are trying to help in some way, it is very easy to "play God" and unnecessarily take their autonomy away from them.

Without knowing the specifics of your situation, let me phrase your question this way: What do we do when we have wronged someone?

Your question begins, I think, at the appropriate place. Reconciling the relationship is the most important goal. This, of course, means that there is no uniform rule to follow because people differ in their reactions to such circumstances. Reconciliation is always a two-way street, and some people will be more open to it than others.

The first step toward reconciliation is to recognize the wrong. While we may wish to justify our actions or make excuses for what we did, we alone are responsible and we must face that reality. It is often said that the biblical sense of the word "sin" is to "miss the mark." This is not, however, like shooting an arrow, when most of us don't expect to hit the bull's eye. While sinning is human, the nature of a sin implies that we could have done the right thing yet chose not to.

Therefore, we must ask ourselves why we did not do the right thing. It's usually easy to find circumstantial rationalizations for why we err in human relationships, but it is better to ponder upon the inner motivational reasons why. This process is best accomplished in a prayerful attitude of self-examination. For example, in the context of your question, one might ask, "Why did I not ask myself how I would feel if someone else were making decisions for me without my knowing?"

There are many possible answers, usually rooted in fear. We fear the person will make our life more difficult by making what we perceive is the wrong decision. Because we are care-givers, we have to be involved in the implementation of the decision, or clean up the mess afterward. We try to make our own lives easier by making decisions which suit our needs, and sometimes lose sight of the feelings of the other person. Such care is, in the end, selfish.

But we can learn from our mistakes. The wonderful thing about God's love for us is that when we fail and turn to God for forgiveness and renewal, we wind up not where we began in our ability to love, but better for the mistake. This is the meaning of the word "redemption." God takes a liability and turns it into an asset.

In Christ, God took one of the worst of human sins, a community's collective, premeditated torture and murder of an innocent man upon the cross, and transformed it into a symbol of love and glory. The message of the cross is that God has received our sins in the pierced body of Jesus and invited us to have the courage to face our complicity even now by the ways we hurt one another.

166

Finally, if possible, we must be willing to make it right. Of course, the courts are full of cases where the issue eventually becomes what is to be done to make the situation as right as possible. There seems to be a consensus that punishment somehow makes things right. Punishment may gave a deterring effect, but even this is highly debated. It never reconciles.

Restitution is in order, and should always be made, if possible. But even if restitution is possible, remember, the goal for people of faith is reconciliation. All of our efforts to deal with our hurtful actions must not be primarily focused upon easing or minimizing our guilt, but rather upon increasing our awareness of what we are capable of, deepening our sense of God's forgiveness and working toward restoring a sense of wholeness in our relationships once again.

*I know as a Christian that I
must forgive, but I just can't. How does one get to a
place in his heart where forgiveness is possible?*

From what you have told me, you are stuck between your pain and the guilt of not being able to forgive. Forgiveness is, indeed, at the core of Christian spirituality, yet genuine forgiveness must come from a certain place within us that contains gratitude.

People try to forgive others for a variety of reasons. In your case, you seem intent on forgiving because you feel obligated to do so as a Christian. This is the motive of guilt derived from a sense of duty. We are paying lip service to forgiveness when we are motivated in this way. Sincere forgiveness comes, of course, not from obedience to teaching, but from inner conviction.

Inner conviction may not come easily, as you have discovered. Until it does, it is important to admit that you do not feel forgiving, and to act as though you did. We can control our words and our behavior so that we respond to Christ's command to love, to act for the good of others, rather than reacting from the pain we are holding. This gap between our actions and our feelings becomes the focus of our spiritual homework.

Sometimes the feeling comes when we are obedient in this way. Faith is not always a matter of feelings. It is not that we act disingenuously, but that we override our desire to take revenge by our desire to serve God and to acknowledge our acceptance of the imperfection of others. Heartfelt forgiveness may even rush into us when we find that God's grace gives us the power to do what we are called to do.

Another reason people try to forgive others is to change them. This, too, is not sincere forgiveness. In abusive situations, for example, the abuser often experiences remorse immediately after an episode. The person abused, desperately wanting to believe that the remorse is sincere and lasting, responds by offering forgiveness. Neither the remorse nor the forgiveness in this scenario is real; it is a manifestation of the dangerous game these people are locked into. The victim offers forgiveness in order to change the relationship. If the victim could arrive at a place of true forgiveness from the heart, it would be a powerful impetus to get out of the relationship. Counseling is vitally important in order for the victim to find the inner strength and self-esteem to put the abuser in the appropriate perspective. Forgiveness is never a justification for allowing continued abuse.

The relationship between Jacob and Esau in the Book of Genesis (Genesis 27 - 33) is one of the foundational teachings in Judeo-Christian tradition about forgiveness. Jacob has stolen the birthright and the inheritance of his brother Esau. Esau is justifiably angry, and vows to kill Jacob. Jacob flees the land and they do not meet again for many years. Meanwhile, Esau has become wealthy and powerful in his own right, and Jacob is understandably fearful of their reunion. But Esau rushes to meet him and embraces him, kissing him with joyful tears. The key to Esau's feelings lies in his response to Jacob's proposal of gifts, "I have enough my brother, keep what you have for yourself." Esau did finally accept Jacob's gifts in order to please him, but clearly had forgiven Jacob before the gifts were offered.

Esau's forgiveness came because he felt blessed by God. What God had given him more than compensated for what Jacob had taken away. His gratitude made the reunion with a lost brother more important than the recovery of stolen property. Restoration of the relationship superseded the justice of punishment for the loss.

The key to unlock heartfelt forgiveness is a grateful heart.

When we are truly appreciative of what God has done for us by giving us life in all of its abundance, we can more easily put our losses in perspective. When we deeply value the magnitude of forgiveness from which God reaches out to us through Jesus Christ, we can more genuinely forgive the offenses of others. When our hearts are filled with the knowledge that we are loved by God, and important in God's scheme of creation, then we are more naturally able to let go of deep resentments.

When Jesus breathed his spirit into the disciples in the Upper Room, giving them the authority to forgive, he was not giving them a franchise. Rather, he was pointing out that the only true authority for forgiveness is our gratitude for God's unconditional love.

We are expected to forgive in all circumstances. I find this terribly hard to do. People sometimes are so cruel that I believe they never cease their bad or negative activities if they are forgiven. What to do?

Forgiveness is the power of Christian living. You say that we are expected to forgive, but I would say we are invited to forgive. This is because our forgiveness is modeled upon God's forgiveness of us. Jesus proclaimed God's forgiveness not because it is right, but because God loves us. Righteousness, from a legal point of view, demands that God banish us, but God refuses to let us go. Love is not rational or legalistic; it is forgiving. It refuses to admit defeat. It is forever hopeful of restoration. It is patient. God is love.

You are invited, therefore, to forgive as God forgives you. The best way to resolve your dilemma is to try to see forgiveness as an opportunity to be faithful rather than as dutiful obedience. If you try to forgive because you feel you are commanded to, you will fail. If you try because you think it is the right thing to do, you will fail. If you try because you want to effect change in the other person, you will fail. Efforts to forgive based on these motives do not extend true forgiveness.

But if you choose to forgive because you believe the other person is a human being and therefore precious to you and to God, you will be starting from a better place. This may be an act of faith, at first. One does not generally feel that an offender is precious. You have to work at it.

Even if it doesn't happen (and it will take some level of repentance by the offender or a new understanding on your part for it to happen) your actions have been spiritually healthy for you anyway.

Forgiveness is the fruit of love. Where there is no love, there can be no forgiveness. The kind of love of which I speak, of course, is not romantic love, or the natural love of one another, but God's love. Forgiveness is the fruit of that love, and love is the fruit of faith. That is why forgiveness is an act of faith.

After examining one's motive, it is important to examine one's actions. Our actions are often driven by feelings of revenge and anger, which trap both us and the offender in the offense, rather than in the power of God to heal and restore.

Most of the figures of the Bible were people with major flaws when God called them. Moses, King David, and Paul had murdered or been an accomplice in murder, for example. God took them as they were, helped them to feel the pain of the actions, and invited them, nonetheless, to be leaders of God's people. God restored them through forgiveness, and God does the same today. Messengers of forgiveness can be the ones whom God uses.

Forgiveness does not mean tolerating or enabling hurtful or unhealthy behavior. Regarding alcohol or drug abuse, for example, the loving thing to do is to require responsibility and accountability for the actions and neglect which the abuse fosters by not letting it continue with you. This is a hard road to travel. It is as hard on the loved ones of an abuse as it is on the abuser himself. It is indeed, tough love. But the pattern of cooperation which prevents the abuser from being accountable must be ended.

You say that forgiveness does not seem to change behavior, but I can tell you that a spirit of forgiveness that embodies both cherishing the person and exercising tough love can lead to a change in behavior. Though the abuser may seek out other enablers for awhile, such a strong message from loved ones has a profound impact over time.

*My brother wants me to in-
vest with him in a Christian bookstore. He says it is an
act of faith, but I choose to judge it by its economical
potential alone. Am I not being faithful?*

Knowing your brother, only you know how big a leap of faith he
is asking you to make! Sounds to me like he's manipulating
both his faith and yours toward his own interests. You are right to
use your best financial judgment. When we exercise responsibly
the gifts God has given us, we practice our faith.

I don't know the statistics of Christian bookstores, but I suspect they are as risky as other new small businesses, 80 percent of
which fail within five years. There are many other personal factors to consider. Going into business with a sibling also puts at
risk good feelings between you and your brother. This reality increases the stakes. Ultimately, such decisions are best made knowing you can afford to lose the money, and deciding that such a loss
would not harm familial relationships.

Your question raises the deeper question of faith. What is it,
exactly? In Hebrews 11:1 we are told that faith is the assurance of
things hoped for and the conviction of things not seen. Traditionally, people have taken two divergent paths in response to this summary of Biblical faith.

Faith communities believe that revelation from God is set
forth in doctrinal statements based upon the authoritative interpretation of Holy Writ; for Christians, the Bible. The faithful are
invited to trust in the values of the larger community.

Here is where the one path becomes two. Some take the path
of certainty. Others take the path of ambiguity. Those who choose
certainty tend to articulate the faith in highly detailed and inflex-
ible ways. Prone to be dogmatic and literal in their interpretations, they see clear distinctions between their faith community
and the world around them. Their faith is static and harkens to
traditional values. Such certainty gives a sense of security and
fosters a uniformity of purpose which can serve our human need
for belonging and finding ultimate meaning in life.

The other path of ambiguity holds to tenets of faith broadly,
allowing for a diversity of interpretation. Those who choose this

path tend to aver basic truths while preserving the mystery of God. They value a diversity of viewpoints and generally seek to engage the world in substantive dialogue, both to evangelize and to hear God speak from the outside. This path offers security through the ability to find peace in the world without isolation. It is dynamic and forward looking.

You may say that both paths are necessary to a healthy faith position. Certainty without ambiguity leads to fundamentalism; ambiguity without certainty leads to subjectivism. Ambiguists see certaintists as arrogant and dogmatic, while certaintists see ambiguists as unbelieving and relativistic.

Robert Frost immortalized the superiority of the path less traveled. Jesus spoke of the narrow door. When it comes to matters of faith, the path less traveled and the narrow door is the one of ambiguity. Apart from Jesus, the biblical archetype is Abraham. He didn't know where God was leading him, yet he turned from the certainty and security of this familiar world toward the unknown future. Abraham needed to let go of his existing value system to be engaged dynamically by the living God. The fact that he could do this, even when it appeared that God was asking him to sacrifice his son Isaac, makes Abraham a defining figure in faith history.

In most decisions of life, the path of faith is the path of letting go rather than hanging on.

My pastor is leaving our denomination because he cannot go along with some of the things going on today in our church. He is urging those of like mind to follow him. I love my church. Can you give me some guidance?

You are describing a phenomenon which occurs in many churches that tolerate diversity. Clergy and laity leave for conservative churches where they will not be confronted with practices which they feel violate biblical and traditional Christian stands.

Virtually all of the traditional mainline Protestant churches, such as the Methodist, Episcopal, Presbyterian and Lutheran, have been torn apart by issues of authority, contemporary and inclusive language, women's ordination, homosexuality, and abortion. National church leaders generally seek to facilitate debate while holding their denominations together under the banner of "inclusiveness." Yet, some members are dismayed by what they perceive as worldly values gradually and inevitably eroding ancient positions.

The question you must ask yourself is what kind of faith you seek.

Do you expect your faith to urge you to assess established truths in the light of today's information and perspectives? To embark upon this journey is to take the path of uncertainty and newness. It does not provide worldly security in the form of constants we can trust. The words and even the positions of your church may change because there is ongoing debate upon matters of worship, authority and biblical interpretation. You have to ask yourself whether you have the stomach for ongoing turbulence. If your faith demands certainty and the orderly peacefulness of authoritative leadership, you might want to follow your pastor.

Do you expect your faith to perceive God's revelation from outside the church as well as from its own tradition? Tolerant churches learn from what they perceive as the movement of God in the world. The women's movement, for example, has transformed some churches while causing others to dig in their heels. In the past it may have been science, anti-slavery or civil rights issues or the peace movement. Your present church will continue to be slowly influenced by the Holy Spirit working in the world because it is listening for God. If you want a church which is open to God's voice apart from its own traditions, then you will want to stay where you are.

Do you expect your faith to require you to reach out to the broken world around you, welcoming the stranger, the disenfranchised, the sinner and the hurting one? We are naturally afraid of people unlike ourselves, and their presence brings into question some of the values upon which we base our own lives. It is not easy to discern which of these values is truly of God and which is merely of our own tradition. It is easy to condemn homosexuality, for example, when one is a heterosexual. It is far more challenging to reach out to a homosexual in love and allow him or her into the life of the church which seeks to help all of us live our sexuality more responsibly and lovingly. If you want to sit next to people who may have a different perspective from your own and see themselves in the process of becoming whole rather than having arrived, stay where you are.

Aligning ourselves with a church where there is no debate upon serious issues, very little change, and increasing isolation from the world, almost guarantees that we will not be challenged to change. Yet there are times when the Holy Spirit leads us to confront ourselves. It's always difficult to know when that is, but if you want to ask the question once in a while, then don't follow your pastor.

It is very discouraging to me that people in my church can be so unloving at times. I tell myself that this is not the way we are supposed to be as Christians, and I wonder if all churches are that way. Are they?

C hurches consist of people, and people are unloving at times. Our expectation is that a church is a place worthy of our trust, where people love one another the way God loves them. The truth is that a church community can contain all of the power struggles, turf wars and oppressive attitudes which exist wherever people gather together.

In some ways, church communities can be more difficult than other types of organizations. A church does not normally turn difficult people away. On the contrary, a healthy church is one that is willing to tolerate misfits, welcome strangers and love the unlovable. This sounds well and good, until we realize that people are unlovable for a reason.

Another explanation of why churches can be difficult is that cherished traditions are easily threatened by new ways of thinking. We tend to cling to those forms and structures which have brought us healing and renewal, and resist any attempts to try new ones. People may give the impression that they welcome new ideas while actually bucking their implementation.

This creates a feeling of hypocrisy and disappointment within those who seek to create activities relevant to their own needs. New people sometimes find it impossible to "break in" to the power structure. While the elders are delighted to have younger people around, for example, they want them - and their children - in their place.

Finally, churches can be difficult because our expectations are so high. Even when a church is loving to its regular members and newcomers who think they have found a nurturing, spiritual home, as soon as they get involved in committee work or leadership, they discover the business of running a church to be a very unspiritual experience. Some are devastated because they thought becoming a leader would give them an even deeper encounter with God's love.

If all of this sounds as though my opinion of churches as loving communities is not very high, that is not the case at all. Rather, it is simply that we do not learn how to become a loving community until we have made our peace with the reality of an unloving world - including the church community.

You see, a church is where we can learn to go beyond, rather than avoid, the ways we hurt each other. When you feel offended, you have an opportunity to experience the Kingdom or to reject it. It is only when there has been an offense that forgiveness and reconciliation come into our human experience - if we work toward that end.

It is only when we observe in ourselves and others the contrast between our actions and the love we are called to by Jesus that we can sincerely repent and move forward, this time less on our own strength and more in the grace and power of the Spirit. In other words, we learn from our mistakes, but we must make them to learn from them.

A Christian community consists of people who do not depend upon positive experiences in order to stay together. Rather, we depend upon the love of Christ. Of course, we strive to make our churches bearers of Christ's love, but we know that when we fail, our focus upon Jesus will heal us and reconcile us to those with whom we feel broken.

The hope for peace in the world does not lie in the possibility that human beings will ever become perfect and never hurt one another. Rather, the hope lies in the possibility that when we do hurt another person, or they hurt us, that we will seize the moment to experience asking for and offering forgiveness.

Such attitudes can only grow from a strong faith in God and an ever deepening trust in the love of Jesus Christ. When we think of our churches as places where we learn how to forgive rather than places where we learn how to be perfect, we are less vulnerable to being disappointed in them.

SOCIAL ISSUES

*What can we do to instill
moral values in our young people? The alarming use of
drugs, teen sexual activity, and gang violence indicates
to me that morality just isn't getting across to today's
youth.*

W e're all concerned for the future of our young people and our
country. There's been an alarming decline in values which
we have known to be necessary for healthy communities. Those of
us who are parents know the frustration of doing our best and still
feeling that we are losing ground.

Here's a thought for you. When I was in the eighth grade, I
learned about the Bill of Rights. I never learned about the Bill of
Responsibilities. Did you?

None of us did. That's because there is no such thing, but
maybe there should be. We have made sacred individual rights
and yet ignored the individual's responsibility back to the community. Court case after court case expands individual freedom of
expression and right to protection from the community, while the
obligations inherent to a free society are largely ignored.

In the absence of common values, freedom degenerates into
chaos. It is impossible to write sufficient laws to govern behavior
when a visceral sense of decency is lacking in the community.

How should we instill values? Because the public schools are
where the majority of our citizenry receives not only education but
the ability to relate to people who are different than themselves,
this is the obvious place to begin. Of course, it is hoped that values

are instilled at home as well. A small percentage of our children may also receive it from our churches and synagogues.

But even these influences are often mere extensions of the supremacy of individual rights. It is in the public arena where children must learn to cope with the diversity of our society and learn to relate in healthy ways not only for themselves but for the whole community. It is there where society's values must be taught.

If we don't we will become increasingly dependent upon laws and the criminal justice system to protect our quality of life. As we are experiencing, this is a downhill slide.

Now the point of contention, of course, is this: Whose values should be taught? We assume that we could not, as a community, agree on a set of values. I believe this is a fallacy. Such values still widely exist. They are usually exemplified in the conduct of our public school teachers, who try to impart healthy social attitudes and build students' self-esteem. We need to articulate those values in a curriculum designed for every age group to be instilled in our children every year of their public education. They need to learn from the earliest ages that freedom is only as good as the attitudes we hold toward one another.

So here's a stab at expressing the common values upon which we all could stand:

1) Respect one another. No two people are the same, and it is important to allow each person to grow into the fullness of their lives. It is also your responsibility to be accountable for your own life as a precious human being.

2) Tell the truth and try to be honest with yourself. Your feelings are important. Integrity is the most valuable asset you can have.

3) Do good for others. When you help another person, you are helping yourself and those you love.

4) Learn from your mistakes. Mistakes are a part of life. When you hurt someone, or yourself, let the experience make you wiser, humbler, more compassionate, and less judgmental.

5) Let your actions express what you truly believe. Actions speak louder than words.

6) Be a friend to others, even to strangers, but do not allow yourself to be victimized if you can help it. Friends tell others when

they are being abusive and do not tolerate it.

7) Try to give without expecting something in return. Then when you receive, it will truly be a gift.

8) Take care of yourself physically, emotionally, and spiritually. When you depend upon others for your wholeness, you are surely going to be disappointed and find yourself in unhealthy relationships.

9) Participate in the community in which you live by bringing your particular point of view and unique gifts. Your offering adds to the richness of the community.

10) Work together with others to improve the quality of life of all. True freedom, justice, and peace are qualities in life we strive for by honoring one another and helping one another to achieve them.

We're in a lot of trouble in the world today. We have lost definite values in the effort to be politically correct. All truth is relative to the individual, with one person's truth just as good as another's. Your writing encourages mutual respect, but where are the solid values necessary to hold society together?

I hear the anxiety in your question. There is a values evolution underway that started in the 1960s and has found expression in each of the decades since. As we prepare to break through to the next millennium, it is time for the elders of society - theologians, pastors, teachers, parents, and yes, politicians - to accept the responsibility of leading us forward.

To date, we are still rebelling from the values which many have experienced as chains of slavery. Rules are always going to be enforced by some and resisted by others. A society based entirely upon rules is difficult to sustain because it divides people between those who obey and those who don't. It is held together by the enforcement of the rules.

Of course, we must have laws in any society. But we need leadership to take us beyond the law as the standard for our relationships and our behavior.

What we currently see in the values arena is a strong call to return to the values of yesterday. Several best-selling books challenge us to return to virtuous living. In the Christian community, we hear the call to hold on to the values of the past from a conservative pope and the new movements in the evangelical communities which challenge men to take their "rightful" role as heads of families.

In society at large, it is tough talk from politicians which gets our votes as we desperately write tougher enforcement into our laws and fill our prisons faster that we can build them. Yet, none of us feels safer.

Wanting to return to the past is part of what it is to be human. The Bible describes such a time when the Israelites were set free from Egypt and led by Moses into the wilderness. Because it was a time of uncertainty and fear, there was an overwhelming desire to return to the old yoke of slavery, because they at least knew what the rules were.

But God, through Moses, led them forward until a new way of being as a people was defined through their struggle. The Ten Commandments were given as God's prescription for life's blessings. Later, while the people had God's spokesmen in judges (male and female) to rule them, they nonetheless wanted the certainty of kings, like their neighbors.

Rather than being open in spirit to the guidance of God, they preferred earthly authority. So God gave them what they wanted, a king, knowing that they would have to learn that security is not a matter for earthly rules, but of the heart, in relationship to God and humankind.

While I can't predict the future, there are some indications of what it may look like, if we are willing to let go of the old ways, and it is far superior to the past. First, accepted norms will transcend national and cultural boundaries. With nations able to destroy each other easily and with the age of information, national barriers are falling whether we like it or not. There will be a flexibility which will honor the diversity of humanity while focusing upon the values which hold it together.

Second, future norms will be less hierarchical. The rigid patriarchal ways of establishing order in the past will give way to a more fluid and subjective way of being more obedient to the Spirit of goodwill and mutual caring. We will be less dependent upon enforcement and more reliant upon internal levels of trust, respect, and integrity.

Finally, there will be more empathy and compassion. We will honor one another and work toward the inclusion of all people in the blessings which life has to offer.

This vision of the future may be recognizable. It is the love of God made manifest in the world. It is time - past time - that our leaders in the faith communities articulate this future hope rather than sound the alarm to return to the past.

Would you please say more about religious abuse? You've referred several times to such abuse, and I'm not sure what you mean.

I consider abuse to be anything which diminishes the dignity of another human being. It is at its worst when there is an imbalance of power. We are outraged, for example, when adults abuse children, and concerned when people in positions of power abuse their authority.

In biblical terms, abuse can be seen as the antithesis of "agape," the biblical word for the kind of love experienced in Jesus Christ. Agape seeks to do what is truly helpful for the other person. It contains a sacrificial aspect because ego-centered benefit is set aside in order to be helpful. It is not taking for one's self, but self-giving for another. It is not exploitation, but nurture. Such love brings life into the world, while self-centered forms of behavior, even when called love, bring death into the world. We have a clear choice: life or death, and the word of God invites us to life.

Religious communities can be abusive. Religious communities - all of them - are subject to behavior motivated from fear rather than faith. They need to be on constant guard of judging others, defensive condemnations, and inappropriate use of the power given to them. Members of religious communities have a right to be free from manipulation through the implantation of fear or the false promise that salvation is the result of their particular rites and creeds rather than the promise of the love of God.

183

Religious traditions point to the true love of God, and to this degree they can be bearers of that love. They are not, however, the sole bearers of God's love. We become abusive when we think we are the only franchise for God. We demean not only those who are not part of our "in" group, but also those who are, because we divert them from true faith in God to faith in our institution.

Children are abused with such ideas, which makes it particularly sinister. They routinely learn, for example, that they are inherently evil and that God is going to destroy them if they don't believe in the teachings of their particular community. Even worse, God will torture them eternally if they don't become good and faithful members of their religion.

They may learn that the world is dominated by evil creatures from whom they need "divine" protection, administered by their group, of course. They may be taught that their religion has the only true knowledge of God and that others are their enemies because they see God differently. Children are taught the "rules" by which they achieve acceptance from God, and live in constant fear that they may transgress one of those rules. Of course, they do break the rules as they grow up. This reality creates either denial of the truth and judgmental projection upon others, or a deep-seated sense of shame from which it is very difficult to recover.

People of faith need to be acutely sensitive to abuse done in the name of God. We know how destructive all forms of abuse can be to our emotions, our self-esteem and our sense of community.

Unquestioned abusive behavior from our religious communities can also do great damage to our spiritual lives.

Would you please respond to the Pope's recent letter which reemphasized his negative position on women becoming priests? I find this rigid point of view quite appalling.

It would not be appropriate for me to comment specifically on the Pope's decision because I am not Roman Catholic. I am happy, however, to address the general issue of women in the clergy.

Decisions such as these are based upon the Bible, tradition, and reason. Churches may place more emphasis upon one of these

184

than the others. Some churches view them as an interrelated whole and try to hold them in balance.

For Christians, the Bible witnesses to a gradual unfolding of the will of God which comes to its most definitive expression in the person of Jesus Christ. With regard to women, the Bible affirms the role of women as ministers of God's love.

Of course, it was a woman who brought Jesus into the world (Mary). It was a woman who first acknowledged his identity (Elizabeth). It was a woman who received his first healing (Peter's mother-in-law). While twelve men are listed as disciples, we know that women were followers of Jesus, too.

Only the men are cited for traditional and symbolic reasons (there were twelve sons of Jacob in the Hebrew scriptures). The women proved faithful to Jesus at the cross while his disciples (except for John) deserted him in fear. After the resurrection, Jesus first appeared to women.

These are just some of the examples of biblical women as powerful instruments of God's revelation. Considering the male-dominated social structures of ancient times, the Bible represents a radical upheaval of the traditional roles of men and women. The overriding message is the partnership of male and female within the context of the love of God. Role distinctions and hierarchical relationships are dissolved by the transforming power of God's call to life and ministry. St. Paul generally taught submission to the social order of the day because any context can provide opportunities for witness to the love of God. It is clear in his theology, however, that in Christ there is no male or female.

With regard to tradition, there is evidence that women were effective leaders in the life of the early church, but this did not prevail in the development of church order. It was simply too radical a notion, and the church succumbed to the dominant social order. It has taken two thousand years and God's revelation through the civil rights movements to awaken churches to even consider the question of the ordination of women. Tradition is hard to overcome, and rightly so. We know, however, that the fact we have always done it that way does not make it God's will.

Finally, there is reason. Reason allows us to draw the conclusion that the essential qualities of the love of Jesus have nothing to do with the fact that he was a man, any more than the fact that he was Jewish or a native of the Middle-East. The incarnation is necessarily time, place, and gender specific, but its revelation is for all times, all places, and both genders. Unless we are willing to conclude that God is equated with maleness (and people do, witness the furor over the recent Image of God conference in Philadelphia where some female images of God were used), there is no rational reason, in my opinion, why women cannot perform pastoral roles in church leadership.

There is good reason to include both male and female models in priesthood. The priesthood, after all is supposed to be exemplary of humanity, not just male humanity.

> *It is very clear to me in scripture that homosexuality is a sin. How can anyone who is a Christian support such a lifestyle?*

This is one of those questions which can best be addressed by returning to the three-legged stool of scripture, tradition and reason as our basis for an answer.

Yes, some Christians believe that homosexuals can live with integrity and sexual intimacy in a committed relationship while fulfilling their call as Christians.

Scripture holds many taboos in both the Hebrew and Greek Testaments. One of these is homosexuality. On the basis of scripture alone, however, it is difficult to say that homosexuality is sinful because we have a long tradition of picking and choosing which taboos of scripture are God's will in the contemporary era.

For example, the Book of Leviticus is often quoted as the last word on homosexuality, yet Leviticus also contains other instructions which even the most ardent fundamentalists choose to ignore. It endorses slavery, sets forth rules for the sacrifice of animals, prescribes capital punishment for blasphemy, the stoning of prostitutes, and even the burning of the daughter of a priest who curses her father, to name a few.

On the other hand, today we are more severe than the Levitical code with regard to other matters, such as adultery. In Leviticus, adultery was a property issue. It was understood that men could have more than one woman, even in marriage, and the law addressed the issue in the context of violating the rights of another man.

Sexual fidelity in marriage was prescribed for a woman, but not for a man. Our secular laws today may not pay much attention to adultery, but no one I know thinks it's acceptable behavior.

Tradition is rife with examples of adding to or subtracting from Biblical instruction. We no longer accept slavery. Women and children are not considered property. The mandated celibacy of clergy was not added until the 12th century. Jesus himself is recorded in the Greek scriptures as seeing through the legal codes to the spirit of the Law. The social roles of men, women, and children have all been in a constant state of evolution as we move toward trying to live the truth of the liberating words and example of Jesus in each generation's own day.

Speaking of Jesus, he never said anything about homosexuality, so far as we know. His silence is remarkable, considering how much he said about other things, such as the use of money, dealing with fear and intolerance, and the urgency of loving one another as we are loved by God.

From the perspective of both scripture and reason, then, it seems clear that while scripture and tradition condemn homosexual behavior, it is also clear that both scripture and tradition provide ample precedent for the spirit to overrule some specifics of the scriptural legal codes as history unfolds.

This leaves the rational considerations. Here we must be aware of the prejudice held against homosexuals by heterosexuals. Many people hold the idea that to be a homosexual means that one is over-sexed, lewd, promiscuous, and a pedophile. They believe that homosexuals are out to convert young people to their lifestyles. The facts prove otherwise. The existence of these abuses is no more common among homosexuals than heterosexuals.

We are learning that homosexuality is a given for a certain number of people. It is not what they choose. It is simply the way they are, just as heterosexuality is for the rest of us.

Is it rational that a person can have a nurturing, responsible, committed, intimate relationship with another person of the same sex? Of course it is. Is there a rational basis in scripture for it?

Yes. The essence of loving one another as Jesus loves us demands the qualities of integrity, fidelity, mutuality, nurture and unconditional commitment. For a homosexual person these qualities may be possible only in a homosexual relationship.

While most of our churches have not yet provided official blessing of homosexual relationships, it is clear to me that such leadership from the church is needed if we are to focus on those matters that are truly important to the sexuality of us all.

Jesus spoke strongly against divorce, yet our churches are full of divorced people, and even many ministers have been divorced but are still pastors. Don't you think that the break down of the family is due largely to the casual attitude in society toward divorce, even in the churches?

I don't agree with your premise that there is a casual attitude toward divorce in our society. As a pastor I've been closely involved in many divorces, including one of my own, and I can assure you that none of them was taken casually.

Jesus spoke clearly on the issue. Marriage is a lifelong commitment between a man and a woman which is intended by God for their mutual joy and the building up of society. There is no argument here. Marriage is the most important commitment we can make to another person. It is a primary means of God's grace. Healthy marriages build healthy human beings.

But when a marriage fails, what then? This is when other things Jesus said become important, too. He spoke often of forgiveness. No matter what a person's past mistakes, he offered God's hand of love and encouragement for a new life. There is not one incident of a person who seeks forgiveness and the opportunity to start over again being condemned by Jesus.

We should also remember that the only time Jesus spoke about divorce was when he was asked by males from the male perspective. His response was not only to uphold marriage, but also to place the vows between a man and a woman on an equitable basis. A husband is bound by the same law as a wife, in other words. Jesus re-stated the law of creation, where the two are bound to each other because they are part of one another.

The forces leading to the high rate of divorce are many, but I think at least some of them are positive. There are worse things than divorce. For example, formerly more couples stayed together, while it was generally tolerated for men to have mistresses. Wives were entrapped by the disgrace of divorce and little recourse in the courts. It also used to be that people suffered a lifetime in unfulfilled marriages, often enduring the consequences of spousal or child abuse, substance abuse and other sorts of unhealthy coping mechanisms. I ask you, in these circumstances which is better, the hypocrisy of a marriage or the honesty of a divorce?

Yes, our churches are filled with divorced and remarried people. Thank God they're welcome there, and are seeking the healing and renewing resources that churches and synagogues should provide. Often congregations can supply a sense of continuity and hope desperately needed by couples and their children in order to move through tragic times.

Couples working honestly and openly early enough in their relationship, and in the context of God's love, have a very good chance of a successful marriage. Certainly it is hoped that forgiveness and reconciliation can be central in the ongoing renewal of our marriages. Sadly, many of us have had to learn this the hard way. We can be grateful that God never gives up on us.

Recently I came across a flyer published by a group called "Clergy for Choice" and your name was included. I thought Christians were against abortion. As a priest, how can you be for it?

I am not for abortion. Rather, I am for the right of a woman to choose whether or not to be pregnant. This is a complex issue which divides both Christians and the community at large. It is an issue upon which Christians should seek to overcome division and work with people of other faiths to resolve.

The position of "pro-lifers," as I understand it, is simple: Abortion is the taking of a human life; it is murder.

Why, then, is this a complex issue? First, there is argument over when human cells become a human being. Is it at the moment of conception, or is it at some point during pregnancy? Even those who are pro-choice would agree, for the most part, that the justification for abortion declines as the pregnancy continues. Few are comfortable with abortions after the first three months.

Second, the issue of abortion is complex because many hold that there are circumstances in which abortion is morally justified. The percentage of abortions due to rape or incest, or even for health reasons is relatively small, however. For me, it is never a good or happy choice, but a choice for the lesser of evils.

Abortion should never be taken casually as a form of birth control. People of faith generally believe that loving parents who are committed as life partners provide the best environment for childbirth. When that setting is lacking, whether or not to bear a child becomes a very difficult personal decision on the part of a woman. Her faith, her family and community of support, and her own circumstances in life need to influence that decision. Ultimately, the decision must be hers because she is the one on whom the responsibility will fall as mother of the child.

The fact exists that poor women, minority women and victimized women are largely powerless in our society. Sexual activity for many women is often on male terms, even in matters of birth control. Outside the home, many women find institutions, even churches, dominated by men who make decisions for them, reinforcing their subjugation in society. This is why the abortion issue is often framed within the issues of the rights and responsibilities of women.

Abortion issues should be viewed not only in the context of destroying or preserving a potential human life, but also in the struggle of women for the freedom to make their own life decisions. The daily number of abortions in our society is appalling, but this is due to young people's inability to make healthy choices prior to sexual activity, and not to some innate immorality. The more we help young people to make such healthy choices, the closer we come to resolving the issues of abortion.

Both pro-life and pro-choice people would do well to expend their time and energy in common causes working to reduce the frequency of abortion. We could do a much better job of giving young men and women self-esteem, empowering them to make good choices.

We could do a better job of educating our young people about the social and psychological consequences of sexual activity before they are ready to assume the responsibilities of commitment and of the nurture of another person.

We could be more supportive of organizations, such as Planned Parenthood, that are available to provide education that can both prevent unwanted pregnancies and allow young women to grow up before they assume the role of motherhood.

We can also support those agencies that assist pregnant women who choose to give birth and place a child for adoption.

Perhaps most important of all, both pro-choice and pro-life people could learn to be in dialogue rather than confrontation. We can accomplish far more working together to provide for society's needs and prevent ills than we can through accusations and polarization.

The birth of a baby is not a simple biological matter. If we do not improve our ability to help young people to be whole and responsible, we will continue to have the tragic reality of abortions, or for the lack of that choice, many babies unwanted and unloved.

Don't you think pastors should stay out of politics? A lot of them aren't helping the poor, visiting the sick or preaching God's word. They are so busy worrying about what is happening in Washington. Please tell me where it is in the Bible that a preacher or pastor is supposed to get involved in politics.

There is strong biblical support for the clergy to be interested in politics. The degree of involvement will vary, depending upon the pastoral setting and theology of each minister. Obviously, the Bible does not anticipate the type of government we have in the United States, with our freedom of speech, democratic participation, and representative form of government. So you will not find a specific reference. It is an implied imperative, derived from biblical theology applied to today.

First, one could cite the theology of the Incarnation, and its antecedent in the Hebrew understanding of God. The Judeo-Christian tradition reveals God to be intimately concerned with creation, particularly the role of humanity as stewards of all that God has made. We are called to do our best to respond to God's lead in the ongoing act of creation. The Incarnation of God in the person of Jesus Christ is the supreme expression of God's intimate involvement with the world and invites a human response to God's purposes.

Second, there is the teaching and example of Jesus Christ inviting us to be servants of others. We are asked to find practical ways to express the love of Christ, which was demonstrated so powerfully at the Last Supper when Jesus washed the feet of the disciples. We are expected to be doers of the Word and not just hearers, as the Epistle of James reminds us. This ministry of servanthood does not, certainly, exclude the public sector. While there is much that can be done privately through individuals and service organizations, we also need to do our best to assure that our public institutions are effective in their concern for the health and well-being of all people.

Third, there is a long tradition of using the governmental institution to implement spiritual principles. A brief sketch might include the Hebrew theocracies under the their kings, St. Paul's affirmation of secular governments in the Epistle to the Romans, the Holy Roman Empire, the theocratic cities and nations of the Reformation, and even the protection of religious freedom in our own country. These are all attempts to honor the importance of the spiritual in the midst of the secular. Religion and politics is an uneasy alliance at best, but the reality is that politics is simply too important to be ignored by people of faith.

The role of the pastors in this endeavor is to create an environment within the church which helps individuals to apply their faith to their politics. Each pastor will do this differently, and will have a wide spectrum of opinion on any given political issue. I do not use the pulpit to express a political opinion because I have an unfair advantage. I write my viewpoints on issues, not persons. It grieves me to see Christian leaders viciously attacking individual government leaders. But generally I believe people deserve to know where their pastor and their church stand on the social issues of our day. Members should not be expected to have to agree in order to be in good standing.

You are right, we do not do enough to help the needy and our youth. Without political commitment, however, we will find ourselves and our churches increasingly impotent.

How do you feel about the issue of prayer in public schools?

Sadly, the tendency of well-meaning people to abuse others in the name of God makes it almost impossible to bring God into a public classroom. Fundamentalists are quite varied in what they believe, but they all share one characteristic, the belief that there is only one truth about God: theirs.

I think it is important to teach all children religious tolerance, mutual respect and appreciation of religious differences. Our public schools provide the first opportunity for children to deal with individuals who are substantially different from themselves. Therefore, schools would be an appropriate place to teach religious tolerance and appreciation of others' beliefs.

Without God in the classroom, we are not giving our children a complete education. Human beings have a spiritual dimension. In a Gallup Poll in June of 1994, 85 percent of Americans polled said religion is important to them. Fifty-five percent said it is very important. Our schools can impart to young people the fact that the spiritual life is both very real in human experience and worthy of being honored in ourselves and others. Without such curricula our schools exaggerate the value of material things and subtly nurture the ideal of self-gratification as opposed to a sense of a greater meaning and purpose in life.

We need to teach our children about religious abuse. This issue is at the very core of our foundation as a country. Our forebears came here to escape religious oppression. In turn, some of them became oppressive themselves in the name of God. People of faith have a very poor track record in this area. We must protect young people from such abuse, but we pay a great price by not teaching them a better way.

If we could control those who seek to exploit others, we might be able to do the following: First in lower grades, a time of silence to begin the day is good for the soul. It is a time to pause and be thankful, to pray if that is our way, or to simply relax and center ourselves. The value of quieting the mind and body is well known. We are doing our young people a disservice by not practicing it in our schools.

With a climate of appreciation and mutual respect as a goal for older students, teachers might want to identify the religious traditions of students and allow them to use their religion as material for study, reports, and art projects. This would honor them and their heritage and at the same time educate the rest of the class. Children in the minority would be especially considered and protected from feeling different. The fact is that we are all different, even though we may share a common ground with others.

For children of middle and high school age, field trips to religious centers represented in the community would be appropriate. Religious leaders could be invited to speak at schools to accurately portray their faith and address the tough questions which young people have. The eternal theological questions could be debated, such as, if God exists, why is there so much evil in the world?

Students would be encouraged to seek the resources of spiritual leaders to prepare for such presentations in an environment of honest inquiry. They might even experience what worship is like in differing traditions.

Yes, I know the above is almost impossible because of those who say "My way is the only way." Why do we have to give those folks so much power?

Proposition 187 is causing quite a reaction from religious leaders. What is your input? (Proposition 187 was a 1994 California initiative to withhold welfare and medical benefits from families living illegally in the United States - ed.)

If 187 passes, people are going to be in a very difficult position. Imagine, for example, that you are the principal of a school and suddenly you are legally bound to expel children who do not have proper documentation. Does God discern the needs of children ac-

194

cording to their papers? Would you feel bound by the law of the land? Could you turn such a child and the child's family over to the authorities? How would it feel to you as a teacher to refuse knowledge to a hungry young mind which does not understand the politics of adults?

Imagine that you are an emergency doctor or nurse. Someone is in critical need of care and does not meet the standards of the state. Could you turn that person out onto the street without feeling that something deep within you had died?

Jesus told a story pertinent to Proposition 187, the parable of the Good Samaritan. Jesus responds to a lawyer who, seeking to limit his obligation to be a good neighbor, asks "Who is my neighbor?" The parable describes a Samaritan who crosses all legal and cultural boundaries to help a person in need. The point: No one is unworthy of help when needed.

As a pastor I often encounter people in need. When someone comes for help, we don't refuse them. We do the best we can. We don't make them prove that they are worthy of our help because to do so would undermine the very reason we offer help in the first place: It expresses God's unconditional love. We try to help people take better care of themselves and their loved ones. We try to make sure what we offer is well used.

Yet, we know that we cannot control people's lives in our efforts to love them. They must take responsibility for themselves, and we help them toward that goal.

People in need are in need for a reason. They do not cut the mustard of society's standards. Some have no choice in that reality. Others suffer from the consequences of their own choices. To people of faith it shouldn't matter. We respond to the call within to be compassionate, merciful and as helpful as possible. We trust that such love will have a more positive impact in the life of another person than any scolding or rejection could ever have.

Most people would be appalled if a church asked people to prove their legal status before offering help. People of faith believe their religious communities strive to be models for society, yet many of them will vote for Proposition 187. This is because these are hard times for our state. Many citizens are out of work and the end is not in sight. There does not seem to be enough to go around.

We feel helpless and afraid. The temptation is to betray our faith in God and our commitment to love one another.

Seldom has the ballot box represented such a clear battle-ground with the forces of evil within us.

I served with you on the Monterey County Mental Health Commission, and would like to ask you this question: "What does the cause of mental health have to do with the Gospel and providing pastoral care?"

The mental health medical community has categories of mental illness, but we all suffer from one deficiency or another. While most of us achieve a level of wholeness which allows us to behave in acceptable ways, some are unable to do so due to biological or environmental reasons. From a spiritual point of view, however, we are all lost and dysfunctional without God.

Christians believe that Jesus came to bring God's acceptance of our condition, to be with us in the darkness of our souls, and to lead us to the light of life and love. Faith communities address the human being as a whole person, and seek to incorporate mental health with spiritual and physical well-being.

The Gospel is that every human being is precious to God. Remembering that value is not imparted by worldly success, but by God, we are called to reach out with loving concern to those who fall outside the parameters of what society considers normal. The community is not whole unless every member finds belonging and meaning.

Society rightly requires individuals to act responsibly to-ward others and to care for themselves once they become adults. But when mental illness prevents an individual from responsible behavior, the community can respond in one of three ways. It can isolate such persons by putting them away; ignore them and let them roam the streets letting nature take its course; or it can seek to restore them to whatever level of participation in the commu-nity is possible. A loving community seeks to do the third option which honors human dignity and affirms the community's role in helping one another grow into the fullness of our identity as children of God.

The increasing population of homeless people in recent decades is due in large part to the decrease in resources dedicated to the care of our mentally ill. This has also contributed enormously to our jail and prison populations. It is easy to spend a great deal of money stockpiling people when the funds are available, or to let them roam the streets when the funds are lacking.

As the federal government continues to cut welfare and Medicaid, many will be placed outside the impact of the community's concern. Existing programs of job training, housing, and child care which help marginalized people to attain self-sufficiency will be cut back by the states, who receive federal money for these purposes. California alone stands to lose millions of dollars annually, a shift from federal to local responsibility which cannot be absorbed by our local communities.

We all wish for balanced federal and state budgets. But, is it not more cost effective to provide preventive and empowering resources to move people toward meaningful participation, rather than driving them toward increased marginalization which will eventually lead to astronomical health care and incarceration costs?

Citizens would do well to make sure their representatives are not providing short-term, cosmetic approaches to balanced budgets which will take a terrible toll on human welfare in the long run. We are already reaping the bitter fruit of years of emphasizing the building of jails and prisons, rather than investing adequately in the basic needs of families and children for education and health care.

Our communities have tremendous resources. We can make a great difference simply through our own personal involvement as citizens. No one has ever said that the Gospel is an easy or quick solution to the problems we bear as a community. But if we care, God will lead us to creative solutions.

I am a divorced woman who is living with a man. I have been with this man for 20 years. I was told that it is against God's will and I would not get into heaven because of this. I know it is a sin, but I am bonded to him and don't go out with anyone else. Could you help me get peace of mind on this?

Your friend is wrong. People often think being a Christian means living by a certain moral standard. If that were true, none of us would qualify. Rather, we become Christians through baptism.

Your friend may mean that you are not worthy of calling yourself a Christian because you are "living in sin." Well, your friend is the one who should examine herself or himself with regard to what it means to be Christian.

A Christian is one who knows Jesus Christ and seeks to follow him as Lord. Unlike many modern social issues we face, Jesus spoke directly to your circumstances in the fourth chapter of John's Gospel. While Christians uphold the sanctity of marriage as a means of God's grace, this story demonstrates that Christian love is not confined to marriage.

On his way to Galilee, Jesus is traveling through Samaria. At Jacob's Well in Sychar he encounters a woman who is living with a man who is not her husband. The woman has been married five times and is a Samaritan. She would be considered a sinner on many counts by your friend and by Jesus' contemporaries in the religious community.

Does Jesus condemn her? On the contrary. He invites her to serve him a cup of water, and he discloses his identity to her. She is so moved by Jesus' acceptance of her, even knowing her history, that she becomes an evangelist with no less passion or effectiveness than Andrew and Philip before her in the Gospel.

Jesus broke through the cultural taboos in order to love - and be loved by - this woman. Can there be any doubt that Jesus looks upon you any differently?

On the other hand, Jesus spoke repeatedly against the kind of activity your friend is participating in. He said not to judge others. He said to look at the log in your own eye rather than the sliver in the eye of your neighbor.

And when Jesus was criticized for allowing a woman called a sinner by the Pharisees to express her love for him, Jesus said to them, "I tell you, her sins, which were many, are forgiven; hence she has shown great love. But the one to whom little is forgiven, loves little."

It should be clear by now how Jesus feels about you. Don't worry about what others think. Real friends want what is best for us, and they support us with patience and respect while we discover how best to live our own lives.

Marriage is the unconditional gift of one person to another in the presence of witnesses. It is seeking God's blessing through one's faith community to be filled with and supported by the love of Christ. It is intended to provide the kind of stability and nurture which helps one to grow into the fullness of Christ.

One could say that to marry is the highest honor one can give and the greatest commitment one can make to another person. Nurturing love between two people in marriage is nothing less than a sign of Christ's love for humanity. That's a high calling.

You and others in your situation would do well to ask what might be standing in the way of having for yourselves one of God's greatest blessings. What is lacking in the relationship which prevents you from making that commitment? What hurts and fears prevent you from standing before the altar? Whatever is holding you back is also hurting the quality of your love for one another.

Married persons cannot assume, of course, that to be officially married fulfills their duty to one another and to God. We can live in sin within marriage as well as without. The determining factor is not the certificate, but the quality of the love offered to each other. Christian love is always a matter of the heart, not the ceremony.

I think we should get tougher on crime. Since you were once involved in prison ministry, I'd like to know your opinion.

I was indeed a prison chaplain for a while in my ministry, and helped my church to develop ministry to inmates and their families, and to the victims of crime. I'd like to share with you some things I've learned, drawn largely from that experience and what I know to be the biblical sense of justice.

There are two basic philosophies for dealing with crime - the punitive and the restorative. The most natural of these two is the punitive. Its logic is that if we make the consequences of an offense painful enough, a person will be dissuaded from committing the offense.

Punishment has been the dominant force in our criminal justice system, even in the most liberal of times. And, it is becoming increasingly popular in today's frustrating times.

Punitive justice is doomed to failure because it is dehumanizing. When young persons begin to exhibit criminal behavior they are made to feel unacceptable in the hope that such feelings will turn them around.

Actually, it deepens the root cause of their crime, the lack of connection to community. While incarcerated, they learn to identify with others who are similarly treated as unacceptable.

While corporal punishment is considered unthinkable, what we do to the spirit is far worse. The prisons the public cries out for are little more than factories of anger and abuse for both inmates and their jailers, and more crime is the product.

Most inmates are not violent criminals, and the ones who are, and should be locked up, are not deterred by the fear of punishment.

The other philosophy, the restorative, recognizes that crime is the product of a breakdown in community. When this breakdown occurs, when one person violates another, the task of the community is to address the root causes of that offense and to take positive steps to restore the offending member to a reasonable degree of inner wholeness and ability to live in peace with neighbors.

It also strives to repair harm done to the victim. A phrase which might sum up this philosophy is, "What can we do to make this right and restore wholeness in the community?"

More specifically, restorative justice asks what we as a community can do to meet the needs of our youth for physical and mental health, education, and positive role models? What can the community do to support their families in their efforts to provide a wholesome upbringing?

Such programs are far more cost effective, and serve not only to prevent, but to build. When young people fall into crime, what can we do to treat them with dignity and give them a chance to make it right with the person or persons whom they have offended?

Are the victims of their crime given an opportunity to have their needs met and their questions answered?

We all make mistakes; it's part of being human. We need to let our young people know when they commit a crime that their behavior is not tolerated, but that they are not condemned, and that there is a way to "make it right" and restore their self-respect.

A society involved in restoration rather than fear and retribution becomes a more peaceful society. One local program which does this is the Victim Offender Reconciliation Program (VORP). It trains mediators, people like you and me, to bring offender and victim together to work out a plan of restitution meeting the needs of the victim and giving the offender the opportunity to regain self-esteem.

Usually, the offenders are young people and the crimes are non-violent property offenses, such as theft or vandalism. Cases are referred by the county probation department.

VORP is very successful in preventing recidivism by inviting the offender to take responsibility for his or her actions. VORP empowers the victim by offering the chance to have questions answered and express feelings to the offender. Often, both sides become advocates for one another, and reconciliation and peace result.

Christians seem divided over the issue of capital punishment. At the recent execution at San Quentin there were some pickets with signs saying, "An eye for an eye," and others saying, "Thou shalt not kill." What is your viewpoint on capital punishment?

Many feel that the capital punishment process should be streamlined in order to make it less costly to taxpayers. The legal loopholes and options seem endless in protecting the criminal, and taxpayers usually pay for the defense as well as the prosecution. As pressure builds to cut costs, capital punishment will become more common and consequently more divisive.

We all abhor the act of killing, yet society feels justified when a murderer is killed. Capital punishment appeals to our basic instinct to get even. Ironically, the effect of this is to allow killers to set the agenda for our behavior. Murderers on death row make us all potential killers, albeit through the justice system. If murderers were locked up for life, society would be protected, and they would not pull us down to their level of behavior.

From a Christian point of view, capital punishment is wrong because it is not consistent with the love we experience in Jesus Christ. God's love impels us to view the offender and ourselves in certain ways. First, we are all children of God, not because we are morally pure, but because God loves us. Our value as human beings is neither added to or taken away in the eyes of God because of our actions. This is the meaning of Grace, or unconditional love. All of us are in God's favor because God gives it, none of us deserves God's favor by earning it, and some of us know God's favor by receiving it.

As we have been forgiven, so we must forgive. Nowhere does Jesus teach us to limit our forgiveness to a certain number of chances, or to certain kinds of offenses. Rather, he taught radical forgiveness, even of enemies, to be given as often as necessary.

Forgiveness of a murderer neither means acceptance of the crime nor release from prison. On the contrary, it engages the offender in a life or death struggle. It seeks personal accountability and renewed productivity. Even within the confines of a prison, one can become a contributor to society and therefore, to some degree, be restored to the community.

This leads to the second point, Christian hope. For capital punishment advocates, I would only ask, "Do you think God ever gives up on us?" No matter how discouraging the prospects may seem for a hardened criminal to repent, can we say that anything is impossible for God? It is only in such impossible situations that our commitment to our faith is really tested. The focus ought not to be upon the offender. We cannot control his mind, only his actions. Rather, the focus should be upon ourselves. Are we acting in response to Christian hope in God's love, or are we acting in response to the evil actions of one lost soul? When we execute someone we become what we hate rather than what we love.

Third, capital punishment is wrong because of what it does to society. It not only justifies violence, it sanctifies it. To execute someone is to make a human offering to the god of violence. The murderer becomes the scapegoat. How easy it is for us to think that we have erased our guilt and responsibility by eliminating the bad apple. But God doesn't make bad apples, people do.

Capital punishment is the extreme manifestation of a society that employs violence or the fear of violence as the means of peace and order. Children are kept in line because their parents are larger and more powerful, not because of their trust in their love. Employees are productive because of their fear of being fired, not because they participate in the fruits of their labor. Spouses play the role expected of them for fear that they will not be cared for. And people of faith act morally because they fear the retribution of God (or desire the reward), not because they love their neighbor. A society built upon domination rather than nurture creates criminals faster than we can store or eliminate them.

Some may feel that the scales are balanced when a murderer is executed. But people of faith don't respond to evil with evil. The love of God challenges us to be instruments of life, not death.

> *Do you think Dr. Jack Kervorkian and those who believe in "Death with Dignity" are performing a service to our society, or are they violating the commandment, "Thou shalt not kill?"*

The death of Jacqueline Kennedy Onassis prompted someone to say, "It was a blessing that she died so quickly." We have all heard such things and said them ourselves when people died who faced prolonged suffering. There is blessing in death when the alternative is a tortuous existence which slowly drains life and the welfare of loved ones.

A woman recently told me of her father, ill for decades, who had been brought back from the brink of death through modern medical science, only to face a certain future of pain and incapacity. Her mother is now beginning to show signs of dementia which doctors feel is being brought on by the stress of the ongoing illness of her husband.

Few people these days want such "heroic" medical intervention because they recognize that at such times the healing gift of medicine becomes the administration of prolonged, painful dying.

There was an incident early in the ministry of Jesus which I believe should influence our thinking in this matter. He was preaching in a synagogue when a man with a withered hand was brought before him. It was all a trick to place Jesus in a dilemma. If he healed the man, he would be accused of breaking the law of the Sabbath. If he did not, he would be shown to lack compassion.

He chose to heal the man, and through this event demonstrated his teaching that the Sabbath is made for humankind, and not humankind for the Sabbath.

To help someone who has chosen to end suffering through suicide, when death is certain anyway, is a kindness. It is merciful and compassionate. It is loving.

We need, therefore, to see it as good. Sometimes, in order to be compassionate and loving one must violate a law. It may be a civil law. It may even be a law of God, e.g. "Thou shall not kill." At such times we need to remember that we are not made for the laws, but that the laws are made for us. Most of the time they work for the common good, and should be obeyed. But in individual cases, there maybe times when the spiritual law of kindness and mercy must supersede.

Those opposed to society's acceptance of assisted suicide believe that it deteriorates the sanctity of life. They see a domino effect. First we allowed abortion, now assisted suicide then euthanasia with "quality of life standards" and eventually, genocide. Indeed, when society begins to decide who should live and who should not, we have opened the door to atrocities of which we know human beings are capable.

It strikes me, however, that what Dr. Kervorkian and the "Death with Dignity" movement propose is not that society should determine when death comes, but rather the individual, together with loved ones should make that decision.

Society has already interfered with the natural process of dying through scientific intervention. God heals and sustains life through human minds and hands. Cannot God also show loving compassion through human hands? When medicine can no longer give hope, it seems both natural and ethical for the patient to wish to end the suffering.

Yes, this opens Pandora's Box. There is great potential for abuse. There must be safeguards. I hope vigorous debate on the matter will produce guidelines eventually.

For now, each of us must ask if we would want to be able to make the choice to die on our own terms with dignity and to minimize torturous pain and hopeless medical procedures. I can think of no reason why a loving God would want it otherwise.

Recently I learned that a loved one wanted to be cremated. Frankly, I was shocked. I've always thought that Christians were opposed to cremation, but not sure why. Would you please address this matter?

Cremation is acceptable now in most of Christianity. In 1963 the Roman Catholic Church instituted a form of service for cremation, and in my own Protestant church, The Episcopal Church, there are rubrics which apply when cremation is used. I know other churches allow cremation, and that there are some who teach that it is inappropriate.

Early Christians did not cremate their dead because of belief in the literal resurrection of the body and the expectation of the imminent return of Jesus. The practice became identified with Christianity and repugnance toward cremation spread throughout the Holy Roman Empire due to the Christian influence. By the 19th century, however, cremation began to return as a legitimate option for those planning their "final resting place" or their loved ones.

I officiate at more memorial services than funerals, and cremation is common. While I do not intend to advocate cremation, it is acceptable for several reasons.

From a biblical viewpoint, St. Paul speaks in I Corinthians 15 of a spiritual body, but does not elaborate except to say that it is not of flesh and blood. And the conclusions drawn from the resurrected body of Jesus when he appeared to his disciples and others are ambiguous. His body is identifiable sometimes as when he appeared to the disciples in the Upper Room, but not so when he walks with them on the road to Emmaus or when he appears to Mary Magdalene in the burial garden. His body is seemingly capable of physical powers, such as eating, but also able to vanish from sight and move through solid obstacles. The picture of our resurrected bodies drawn from the Bible is that we will be known, but not because of our physical bodies. As St. Paul says, "Flesh and blood do not inherit the kingdom of God, nor does the perishable inherit the imperishable."

The renewal of environmental concern contributes to the argument for cremation. Space is an issue as our world population increases and resources become increasingly stretched. The piece of earth necessary to indefinitely provide a burial plot comes into question when one looks into a future of limited room for the living, let alone the dead. Good stewardship of the earth means to continue its use in life-giving ways. While it is important to remember our dead and have "markers" by which to honor them, their memory lives on far more permanently in the legacy they leave by their contribution to our lives than in a grave. Cremation allows for less space for burial places, and often no singular burial spot at all.

When an object has been used for holy purposes, it is not simply discarded in the rubbish. Rather, it is traditionally buried or burned. Altar linens, for example, when they are worn out, are burned, and palm crosses used on Palm Sunday are traditionally returned to the church the following year to be burned and become the ashes placed on our foreheads on Ash Wednesday. Likewise, the human body loses its usefulness eventually and cremation honors it as well as its creator.

We have a natural tendency to "hang on" to this world. We mentally and emotionally resist the idea of death and the natural process of the destruction of the body after death. Yet, the Bible tells us that we are dust and to dust we shall return. Nature gives us the same message, no matter how we might try to avoid it through sealed tombs and embalmed remains.

Christian faith tells us that nothing can separate us from the love of God. Our resurrection does not depend upon the manner in which we are buried or how our bodies are disposed of. Our hope is not in correct burial procedures, but in God's grace. While people may have strong feelings with regard to cremation, we can trust that God will give us new bodies regardless of our decision.

The number of humans will double at the current rate to 11 billion around 2034. Even now, 40,000 children die daily from lack of food and irreversible environmental degradation increases. Could you provide some ethical background for universal, responsible reproduction?

The issue you raise is perhaps the most important social issue of our day. Population control must be achieved if other social ills are to be addressed successfully. We can do little to protect the environment, solve problems of hunger and health care, fight crime in our societies, or even establish lasting peace between nations, as long as the human population continues to explode.

In April 1994, the United nations issued this statement: "Runaway world population growth is the most serious threat to local and global environments since the human species evolved."

The world simply needs fewer babies. Education toward smaller families or even childlessness, family planning, contraception and adoption is critical to the solution. People who are better educated and enjoy a higher standard of living tend to have smaller families.

But the inordinate consumption by these families contributes to the imbalance of resources which keeps others poor and prolific. The approach to a solution must be worldwide, yet national pride and self-interest impedes the educational process. Hard decisions must be made which would stabilize population growth through economic and social development and a more balanced resource distribution among all people of the world.

Christian ethics are based upon the teaching of Jesus interpreted to apply to the issues of our own day. Remember, overpopulation was not an issue in biblical times. To propagate one's race in order to assure survival in the competition to populate the earth was an appropriate agenda then.

Not that Jesus ever encouraged anyone to do that, but I feel certain he would have had no problem with families producing as many babies as possible in an age where life spans were comparatively short, infant death rates were high, women's roles were narrowly defined as homemaking, and there was little environmental impact from human population.

The ethical context from a Christian perspective involves the concepts of stewardship, love for neighbor and repentance. The word stewardship simply means that human beings have been given the power and authority to co-create with God the kind of world God intended from the beginning. The environment is a sacred trust, and we have a duty, therefore, to protect and enhance it. Overpopulation destroys the environment. Christian stewardship now calls us to practice restraint in having babies.

Love for neighbor demands that we share what we have with others. It appears from the Acts of the Apostles that the early church taught a communal form of resource distribution, although there is little evidence that it was widely practiced. Generosity, however, has always been a sign of Christian faithfulness.

It is not appropriate for those who have had children and live affluently to preach to others that they must have less. Rather, we must work to develop ways to enable our brothers and sisters in every country and culture to enjoy what we do while protecting what God has given.

Repentance means to look at how we ourselves contribute to the problem and take responsibility for correcting our own lives. Developed countries will need to live more simply. The solution to the world population problem begins with individuals committed to changing their own lifestyles. Such change cannot be forced if it is to be truly helpful. It must come from conviction and dedication to the cause.

Lasting solutions require conversion, not coercion. People who want to know more about the issue may contact Zero Population Growth, 1400 16th St. NW, Suite 320, Washington, DC 20036.

SOCIAL ISSUES

How do you recommend that
people make the personal and collective changes which
humanity requires to survive and how do you envision
such change taking place?

The short answer to your question is that faith in God is the answer. And part of faith is to learn how to accept an imperfect world.

Regrettably people of faith have contributed greatly to the misery of people over history. The historical bloodshed as a result of strong religious conviction has broken down our level of trust. Faith has been used as the vehicle for fearful people to act out their defensive and controlling needs. In the name of God, communities have been divided, subverted, and destroyed.

We people of faith need to change our ways and begin to walk in the paths to which we are truly called. Long ago, the prophet Micah heard the answer to your question: "What does the Lord require of you, but to do justice, to love kindness, and to walk humbly with your God."

It is long past time for us to begin living this way. The words from Micah present a three-fold path of justice, kindness (sometimes translated as mercy), and humility. These are the essentials of wholeness.

We are given choices in the roads we follow. Picture if you will two wide roads and one narrow one. On the left there is the wide road of "anything goes." With few commonly accepted values, the motto is "if it feels good, do it." This road is characterized by a high sense of individual freedom and a lack of accountability to the community or to God.

On the right, picture the wide road of legalism, where morality is exacting, often with divine imprimatur. The individual is forced to comply to the legal code with the threat of punishment or banishment. This road is characterized by authoritative community values intolerant of mercy or compassion.

The narrow road in the center provides community values (a sense of justice), protection of individual expression and nurture (kindness), and a deep reverence for life in both its individual and communal expressions (humility).

To walk humbly with God is to reject both anarchy and legalism. Faith communities must claim their true calling to lead down this narrow road. It is the road of struggle for what is right in the midst of ambiguity.

This journey is an uncertain one. Those who choose this path know only that God is leading. The path proclaims truth even as it learns. It acknowledges the fear we experience when we do what God requires of us, but overcomes fear with trust.

Faith compels us to walk humbly with God and with our neighbor, and not to place limits upon who our neighbor is. If we could live that way, we would go far in curing the world's miseries.

*Someone once told me that if
a person commits suicide, he will not go to heaven.
Would you speak to this matter?*

Suicide is never a solution to one's problems, although it may falsely appear to be the only alternative. Christian tradition has understandably condemned it both in teaching and practice. Clergy have sometimes refused Christian burial for one who committed suicide. I once knew a family whose loved one was not allowed to be buried in a consecrated cemetery. These measures are opposed to the love of Christ, however, and fail in their design as deterrents.

The idea of not going to heaven after suicide comes, in part, from the doctrine of sin. Traditionally, a mortal sin left without the intervening grace of Christ through the sacrament of reconciliation condemns one to eternal damnation. Suicide is murder of one's self, a mortal sin which removes any opportunity for church intervention. The inevitable conclusion, therefore, is that the person will not go to heaven.

Another basis for what you were told is that suicide is the rejection of life, and therefore the rejection of God. The argument says that faith is what one hangs on to when all else fails, and to opt out of this life for any reason is to manifest a lack of faith, and consequently, a lack of the means of salvation.

I believe these conclusions are contravened for several reasons. First, within the doctrine of sin is a distinction between mor-

210

tal and venial sins. A venial sin is one which is less serious and does not represent a barrier to heaven. When a mortal sin is committed by a person who is not of sound mind or in some other way incapable of doing otherwise, the mortal sin becomes a venial sin. I argue that a person in deep depression, confusion or agony of pain is not likely to be in a sound state of mind.

Second, with regard to the issue of faith, we must remember that our faith is not in our ability to appropriate grace, but in God's desire to give it unconditionally. That's why faith the size of a mustard seed will move mountains. Corrie Ten Boom, untiring Christian evangelist was once told she must have a very great faith to travel as she did at such an advanced age. Her response: "My dear, I have a very small amount of faith, but it is in a very big God." A person who commits suicide may not have enough faith to go on, but only a little is necessary in a God who loves as Jesus loves.

The third point is related to the second. Jesus teaches us that our God seeks out the lost. The Good News is not that those who seem to have it all together are the only ones saved. The truth is that there is really no one in that category. Some may appear to be together, when compared to you or me, but not to the glory of God. Yet, salvation is offered to all. Like the shepherd who goes out to find the lost sheep, God will find us in the darkness of our souls. There is no reason to draw the line with suicide. The church may not be able to intercede in this life, but we can trust that Jesus will find a way to make salvation available to the least of his children.

Having said all of this, I must add a word of caution. If you or someone you know is contemplating suicide, there are two very important points to keep in mind. First, suicide is a final and irreversible solution to a temporal problem. While death is permanent, the problem may be transient, or at least potentially seen in a brighter light. Second, our greatest opportunity to grow spiritually comes at the darkest moments of our life. If you are in the valley of the shadow of death, know with the psalmist that God is with you. Reach out for help. Accept the challenge to know God in ways that you have never known before.

We often worry about what's in store for us after we die, but

God's chief concern is how we live in the here and now. It is not a matter of trying to be perfect, but of seeking to grow into the fullness of Christ through our imperfections.

FAITH
AND OTHER VIEWPOINTS

Can Christians be religiously tolerant? I was raised in my mother's faith, Roman Catholic, while my father was Lutheran. My mother was very devout, yet I was brought up with the attitude that respect was due persons with different beliefs. Now, as a "born again" fundamentalist, I sense the more zealous people to be the least tolerant of other beliefs. I'm often chastised for my "lukewarmness."

A Christian ought to be tolerant - and more. As we seek to model our lives upon Jesus, we can learn from his many encounters that he continually confronted attitudes of religious superiority by those who professed that only certain traditions and practices expressed the true people of God.

While Christians have an age-old habit of turning their belief in Jesus into a way to justify acting superior to others, I doubt that Jesus is pleased with this now any more than he was then. He came to break down such ways of thinking.

The truth he brought to the world is that all people are equally precious in the eyes of God. He did not die for some, but for all, and our job as Christians is to continue to convey that good news by treating all people as precious, whether they know Jesus or not. By doing that, we create the best opportunity for the Holy Spirit to speak to their hearts.

One can be passionate in one's Christian faith while respecting those who disagree and those of other faiths. The critical issue is, "What are we being zealous about?" Are we being zealous about the dogma of our tradition, or are we being zealous to love others as Christ loves us?

As Christians it is very important to trust in the truth of Jesus as God incarnate; it is that belief, and only that, which can give us the grace and power to act in a spirit of love. It is this truth which compels us to be the servants of all people, not setting ourselves above them, but rather at their feet.

Because Christ is in us, we can see Christ in everyone, and we evangelize by helping others to see Christ in themselves. If we can't see Christ already in them, how can we help them to?

We need to rid ourselves of the notion that we are the only sacred vessels in which the truth is sprinkled over the world like holy water. Jesus told us that if we wish to be greatest of all we must be servants of all: if we wish to find our life, we must be willing to lose it.

The Judeo-Christian tradition is founded upon two great laws. The first is to love God with all of your heart, soul, and mind, and the other, placed equal to the first by Jesus, is to love your neighbor as yourself. Now, I ask you, is it possible to love your neighbor as yourself while being intolerant?

To love others as one's self means to see them no differently than you see yourself. If you feel that you are a child of God, then so are they. If you feel that you wish more from life, then you will want more for them as well. If you seek forgiveness from your sins, then you will be willing to forgive the sins of others.

To be religious means to live our faith with passion. Such passion for Christians requires that we not only be more tolerant, but also forgiving, accepting, respectful, and helpful.

I would like to have the joy I see some have in a relationship with Jesus Christ, but what seems to go with it is the idea that Jesus is the only true way to God. I just can't accept that. Can you offer me some guidance?

I hear your longing for intimacy with God and a personal relationship with Jesus Christ while respecting the Godliness of other religions. I am often asked similar questions. Mostly they take the form, "Are only Christians going to heaven?"

A passion for Jesus Christ and a respect for the experience of non-Christians are consistent ideas. Christians know that God loves humanity unconditionally. Many Christians accept Jesus as Lord and Savior but seem not to accept his message. We institutionalize Christian faith and confuse the liberating words of Jesus with the constraints of human rules and institutions.

Claiming the gift of God as our own exclusive possession is a human trait that Jesus confronted. This sanctification of pride, greed, and prejudice is rooted, of course, in fear. While intending to express dedication to God, this course, in fact, reveals a lack of trust and a need to be in control.

When the Gospel of John quotes Jesus as saying, "I am the way, the truth and the life; none comes to the Father but by me," it does not mean that God loves only Christians or that only those who become Christian are loved. Rather, it means that God's love for all humanity is greater than any human perception of it.

Our unity with God is God's gift to us. We cannot receive it without accepting its implication that, if given to us, it is extended to all. Jesus taught that we simply cannot make claims upon God by our human traditions. This is no less true of Christianity than it was of his own tradition, the Hebrew faith.

Yes, all gifts must be received in order to be effective. But what does it mean to receive God's gift of love? What does it mean to suddenly feel that one is on the "inside" and those who have not received Jesus are on the "outside?"

Does it mean that there is now a dividing line between Christians and non-Christians? Does it mean that someone from another faith tradition, or with no conscious experience of God at all, is any less acceptable to God?

To be a Christian means to treasure the work of God in all of creation. It requires the willingness to embrace those who experience God differently than we do. It demands that we not reduce God's work in the world by secure, manageable categories.

Jesus is bigger than our efforts to define him. He stretches us to accept even the broken and the unwanted parts of our humanity as precious opportunities for awareness, forgiveness, humility, healing and renewal.

To be a Christian is to be humble about our claims to truth. We believe that God has come to us in Jesus to demonstrate God's love and call to us, but we also know that our human view of Jesus is fallible, conditioned by our finite experience. While we walk on holy ground because of God's grace, we are always open to the holy, albeit unfamiliar, ground which others walk upon, too.

Finally, to be a Christian means to live by the Spirit. This means actively working for understanding between people, the spread of unconditional love and the betterment of life's conditions for all. Jesus' way is to unite people together in the love of God, not to divide or prioritize them.

Jesus invites us to see all people as brothers and sisters, but we don't always want to accept his invitation. The inclusive way of Jesus is hard to hear. It is also hard to live, but for Christian and non-Christian alike, it is God's way.

Would you offer your slant on the Oklahoma bombing?

As has been said by many, evil must not be allowed to defeat us. The evil which lies at the core of the bombing is the way we dehumanize one another.

When we demean another person, we are aiding and abetting evil. It is one thing to disagree. There is nothing evil about that. But when we put people down by name calling, insult, sarcasm, gossip, dishonor or any of the many ways we can hurt someone, we are in league with evil.

Evil is personified in the Bible. The word Satan literally means "Accuser." The accuser makes us feel less than good about ourselves. Jesus, on the other hand, was the advocate for those made to feel less than good. He revealed to us that while God is our judge, God is not our accuser. That is Satan's work. Christians have been entrusted with the ministry of Jesus, to continue to spread the Good News of God's love and advocacy for humanity.

Sadly, evil is quite acceptable in public discourse. While we might criticize the president for political expediency and raising freedom-of-speech issues by suggesting that talk radio is to blame, he is essentially correct that too much of the public dialogue is mean-spirited and destructive of human decency and mutual respect.

Dehumanizing others is subtle, pervasive and deadly. Regrettably, it is also very popular and profitable.

You may take issue with me that the kind of thinking which would lead an individual to destroy lives is in any way connected to the rest of us, our homes and even our churches. Well, we Christians need to look at ourselves. Too much Christian broadcasting has practiced putting people down who do not hold its belief or political ideology. Listen to a Christian radio station sometime, and let them know you do not appreciate programming which tears down people for any reason.

With regard to the Oklahoma bombing, I sat in amazement watching a memorial service - attended by the president on April 23rd - intended to heal, unify and renew hope. Perhaps it accomplished its purpose - for some. Although I did not watch every minute of the service and may have missed something, I could not help wondering how many Jewish or Muslim families sat in quiet resignation as the faith identity of their loved ones lost in the bombing was ignored. Among more than 200 deaths, surely not all were Christian. And even if they were, was not this service intended as a healing for all Americans? The bombing took place in a federal building, after all.

That Oklahoma City is in the Bible Belt of the country perhaps makes the insensitivity understandable. But Christians should be the first to say that something is wrong here. First, people are killed or wounded because of the extreme action of a person or faction, then their value as persons is denigrated - albeit unintentionally - by the larger community gathered together in grief.

Some Christians may feel that the only appropriate service was a solely Christian one. Christ is the way the truth, and the life. But I think Jesus' heart is saddened whenever we devalue others in his name. Unkindness, insensitivity, denial of the validity of other human beings, and the assumption of our own righteousness are all acts opposed to the will of God, and therefore opposed to the spirit of Christ.

The evil which should concern us most does not reside in the minds of those who may take our physical lives, but in our own minds and hearts. The tragic bombing should help us to realize that we can do more to build up our neighbor.

Don't you think the whole of
mankind ought to or must be unified under one reli-
gion? If any would succeed in this, I think peace on
earth would be realized.

The quest for world peace is an ongoing concern for all of us. However, the solution does not lie in religious conformity. I doubt that it is possible, and further, it would not be desirable. Even within single religions peace has seldom been enjoyed. All pastors will describe for you power struggles, petty bickering and division in their congregations. This is human nature. Ironically, it is also part of the blessing of creation.

The struggle for peace needs to be waged not in the arena of religious conformity, but in the arena of tolerance for diversity, caring and respect for those who differ or disagree with us. Faith actively seeks opportunities to learn and grow in the life-giving ways of God. It often manifests itself in strange and surprising ways. How strange it must have seemed to Abraham, the biblical father of faith, when God invited him to pack up and move on to a strange land. Faith kept him moving, and it keeps us moving, too.

Faith does not mold humanity into a homogenous uniformity, but forms a dynamic unity of spirit which rejoices in diversity as it unfolds in the mystery of revelation. At its very best, faith works for the dignity of all human beings, for the common good and for a celebration of life in all of its richness and beauty.

The story of faith through the ages, however, is that it easily becomes the tool for those seeking power. Religious leaders become self-serving, and sometimes with civil authorities become uneasy partners in struggles for control.

We find this struggle in the Hebrew Scriptures describing the period from the first King Saul (1030 B.C.E.) to Zedekiah (587 B.C.E.) where one leader is caught in the tense duality of both king and religious leader. In Christianity, the church was politicized by Emperor Constantine in the Fourth Century who, although not a Christian himself until his deathbed conversion, saw the advantages of making Christianity the official religion of the empire. The church became a significant political institution, but naturally gave its allegiance largely to Constantine rather than to God. This marked the birth of the Holy Roman Empire, an overt expression of the turbulent marriage of political and religious power.

During the formation of the nation states, emerging kings exploited the Reformation for their own political independence. In that time, the alliance of church and state found new, if more fragmented, expression.

The founding of our early colonies was driven by rebellion against the forces of religious conformity mixed with political oppression. Our lasting memory of this era stands as the best protection against a return to one religion becoming "official."

Today we see many examples in the world of the tragic consequences of faith used as a unifying force to perpetrate hatred, violence and political power for the privileged.

This simplified overview of history should make any one disenchanted with the ideal of one world religion. Of course, people of faith need to be involved in the political process, nonetheless.

We need to work for change in order to make humanity more reflective of God's love. This is God's call to us, and God provides both the instruction and the power to make the world that kind of place.

It does not happen, however, in worldly ways through political and religious conformity. Nor would we want it to. It happens through the transformation of the heart responding to the love of God by loving one's neighbor, both next door and across the world.

Why are churches always at odds with one another? Why can't people of different religions, especially Christians, realize that they have more in common with one another than differences? After all, we do worship the same God, right?

Yes, we worship the same God, but from different perspectives, and the problem religions have is thinking their perspective is the only valid one. Maybe we should have an eighth sacrament in the Christian tradition. I would call it humility.

Before saying more about this new sacrament, let me explain for those who may not know what a sacrament is. Traditionally, there are seven, although since the Reformation many Protestant churches have reduced them to two, and some have discarded the concept altogether. The seven in the Catholic tradition are Baptism, Confirmation, Eucharist (Communion), Marriage, Ordination, Reconciliation and Unction (Healing). The word sacrament means "holy mystery." Through these liturgical actions, the church offers its people the ministry of Jesus in the power of the Holy Spirit.

Sacraments can sometimes be seen as the only means of grace. When this happens they lose their sacramental nature, to be signs pointing to and making present the grace of God which is at work, potentially, in all aspects of life. The sacrament of humility would remind church leaders that sacraments are not the only means of grace.

The Imposition of Ashes on Ash Wednesday could easily be elevated to become the eighth sacrament. The admonition, "Remember that you are dust and to dust you shall return" as the ashes are imposed on the forehead is a powerful symbol of our complete dependence upon God and a reminder not to take ourselves too seriously.

Churches stray from their call when the sign of God's grace becomes the property of the church. Sacraments lose their intended meaning when they cease to point to things other than the rituals themselves. Here are some examples. At the Holy Eucharist, or Mass, Catholic tradition holds that the communicant can rely, if the liturgy is conducted in accordance with the canon of the church, that Christ is received. That's why there is such strict adherence to liturgical forms. This ensures the integrity of the sacrament.

Yet, there is no teaching that Christ is received only in the Mass. In fact, sacramental theology teaches that the Mass reminds us of the sacramental nature of all of life. Experiencing Christ in the bread and the wine is a powerful reminder of the preciousness of all of creation as a potential means of the love of Christ. The Mass is the focal point which gives potential meaning to all of the rest.

Likewise, Baptism is a sign of God's salvation and empowerment through the Holy Spirit. How easy it is, though, for churches to say that if you have not been baptized in our particular way that you are not saved. Some of us require a certain age, some immerse, some sprinkle, etc. There are some who believe that salvation is only received through "baptism in the Holy Spirit."

Baptism is meant to be a moment of focus and empowerment to share God's grace with others, but often becomes a means of control and privilege. God's unconditional love suddenly has lots of conditions attached to it.

Many of those who reject organized religion do so with good reason. They see no more than the dogmatism and the control. They may even have suffered from it firsthand in younger years. Our religious institutions do not have to be that way.

To put it more strongly, one cannot proclaim the word of God while in the same breath professing to be its sole messenger. If it is true, it is much greater than our expression of it.

The sacraments are indeed holy mysteries. To preserve both their holiness and their mystery, no human being and no human institution should encompass them. They are offered to build spiritual strength and trust in the God who moves through them. They are not there to "put God in a box."

Yes, the words "Remember that you are dust, and to dust you shall return" are a wake-up call to the church and our controlling and legalistic ways. We have a long history of acting superior to others. Maybe an eighth sacrament would help us act differently.

I was invited to a revival at a friend's church and was shocked at what I heard and saw. People were yelling and screaming, some with strange sounds coming out of their mouths, and when the preacher touched people, many of them collapsed on the spot. My friend explained that they were "slain by the Spirit." I was glad to get out of there. I thought that any minute they would bring the snakes out. What do you think about all of this?

I think it's not for you! What you describe is fairly common in churches which emphasize the literal manifestation of spiritual gifts in worship. These are loosely described as Pentecostal churches because the Holy Spirit was received on the Jewish feast of Pentecost, according to the Acts of the Apostles.

223

Many people experience healing and renewal through such forms of prayer and worship, and while I, like you, am not drawn to it, we would be wrong to condemn it.

We learn some things from Pentecostal churches. First, they challenge the Christian community by their witness to make the Bible more important than other historical documents. While some might not agree with the often literal interpretations prevalent in Pentecostal churches, for all Christians the Bible is the basis for belief and authority. If non-Pentecostals do not necessarily hold that the literal truth is the truth revealed, then in what sense is the Bible the inspired word of God? Pentecostals challenge us to have an answer.

Second, the Pentecostals challenge the Christian community to engage their hearts in their relationship with God. Other Christians may see in Pentecostals a distrust of the sciences when they appear to conflict with established biblical interpretations, the discouragement of legitimate questions which confront traditional ideas, and a tendency to accept supernatural phenomenon with an uncritical eye.

But have those critical of the anti-intellectual Pentecostals abandoned their own simple trust in God? Have they lost their belief in miracles? Have they reduced their faith to a cold intellectual pursuit without the passion of the heart? I fear this is often the case, but it does not have to be. It is entirely possible to remain connected to God at the heart level, deeply moved by the Spirit and emotionally invested in one's relationship with God while fully engaging the inquisitive mind. Both the rational and the emotional aspects of our reality are gifts of the Spirit to us, and we need to strike a healthy balance between them.

Third, Pentecostals challenge us to place God at the center of our lives. We might question their interpretation and application of faith, but their simple trust in God and their willingness to let the Spirit of God consume and direct them reminds all Christians that they are called, essentially, to be Spirit-filled and Spirit-led. Many Christians see the essence of Spirit leadership as loving one's neighbor and working for justice in the world rather than the literal manifestation of spiritual gifts such as tongues, interpretation of tongues, or being "slain" as you described.

Yet, the witness of these literal gifts within the Christian community reminds us that there is more to Christian faith than good deeds. Fundamentally, it is cooperation with God through humble submission to the will of God and creative expression of God's will through the uniqueness of each person's humanity. It truly is a dying to self and rising to the spirit of Christ within us.

Finally, we can learn from Pentecostals that joy ought to permeate our faith. Simple trust, a keen awareness of God's powerful presence and a profound sense of Christ's victory over evil characterize the Pentecostal experience.

Joy can be expressed in many different ways, some less obvious than others, but we have to ask whether the joy of being a child of God permeates our soul? Does such joy permeate our faith community? Does joy make a difference in the way we live? Do we bear fruit in our lives for Jesus Christ because we are overwhelmed with joyful gratitude? Or, have we taken God's gift of unconditional love for granted and allowed the cares of the world and the priorities of its demands to overshadow our greatest treasure, God's love for us and others?

There is a rich diversity of expression within the community of faith. We can learn from one another as long as we respect and honor diversity. We let our Lord down when we expect everyone's gifts and tastes to agree with our own.

What do you think about the New Age Movement? My pastor says it's Satanic. Yet, there are parts of it that are attractive to me. What do you say?

This question is difficult to answer for two reasons. First, "New Age Movement" is a general term for many spiritual and personal growth experiences. It borrows from Eastern religions, the environmental movement, modern psychology, metaphysics, ancient religions and myths, the feminist movement and, of course Christianity. As with all things which are so embrasive, there are certainly some goods and some evils. Second, my inclination is not to be critical of something of which I have very little personal experience.

The role of the Christian Church is not to condemn, but instruct the faithful in discerning good from evil and to nurture them in the practice of that which is good. This means learning about God as revealed in Jesus Christ and being submissive to the Holy Spirit in our lives. Since New Age does not give Christ central and fundamental importance in its varied expressions, I suspect this is why your pastor considers it Satanic.

Your question is really one of authority. By what authority do you make your decision about good and evil? Do you simply believe what your church says (whether it be your pastor or the teaching of the larger church)? Or, is there another way of discernment which will help you to make such decisions for yourself? If you are interested in New Age ideas, here are some tools with which you would wisely proceed as a Christian.

Use these means of discerning the intention of the Spirit. They are: 1) Holy Scripture; 2) That which we learn from the experience of others, now and over history; and 3) The application of reason. Each of these needs to be balanced with the other as we seek to do the will of God while being open to the unfolding mystery of God in our lives. As you grow in each of these areas, you will have the tools to evaluate New Age yourself.

Scripture: The Bible is our first tool of discernment. It is the revelation of God's character in relationship with humanity. It is God's invitation to us to trust in God's life-giving authority and to return the love that God has for us. Christians experience the fullest expression of that revelation in the self-giving love of Jesus Christ. The Bible becomes, then, a means of knowing him because it relates the stories about him, both in the flesh and in the Spirit of Risen Lord, and the saving actions of God with people even before the birth of Jesus. Anything which would be contrary to the kind of love Jesus reveals to us in Scripture should be avoided, and we are invited to follow his example. It is not that the Bible addresses every detail of life, but that overall it reveals the love of God which can be applied to any circumstance at any time. Commonly, Christians give credence to and invest themselves in all sorts of ideas without a solid grounding in Scripture.

The experience of others: We all know that people interpret the Bible in many different ways. Some are literalists. Some try to translate the Bible's meaning of long ago into our own day and age. Everyone, however, is the victim of his or her "personal agenda" in seeking to interpret the Bible. This process of interpretation has been going on, of course, for centuries, and consequently makes up the tradition of the church. We can learn from this tradition in retrospect, both from its obviously good and obviously evil expressions. We can also learn from our contemporaries who are building the present layer upon this rich texture of tradition, whether it be our pastors or the wide spectrum of Christian literature. We can learn from those whom we respect as elders because we sense that they know Christ well.

Reason: Reason is much more than rational process or application of scientific analysis. While these play an important role in discernment, one recognizes that there is much more to human experience than what we can weigh and measure rationally.

Within reason, we include experiences of prayer and the formation of our personal relationship with Christ, ever deepening through our devotions and service. We also include being open to the revelation of God in other religions and God's work in the world outside the witness of our own church. We recognize that part of God's blessing in creation is the gift of both our rational and contemplative minds. Being rooted in our own tradition and Scriptures gives us our identity, but we have much to learn in living this identity with loving integrity in our own lives.

So, what about New Age? That's something you will have to figure out for yourself. I trust that if you immerse yourself in the tools God provides as I have described, then you will not need to hear the answer from me or anyone else. You'll have a pretty good idea of God's will for you. Remember, you are the temple of the Holy Spirit, and have been given the gift of discernment.

Are you a plumbline Christian, or what?

This question was asked of me by a visitor to our community. This was a new term to me. Christians have a knack for figuring up self-righteous names to elevate themselves above the crowd. It used to be "true believer." Then came "born again," "spirit-filled," and "Bible-believing." Now we have "plumbline Christians." Why dont people simply say no one else is Christian except their own kind?

My immediate response to my visitor was to say, "Well, I guess we all think we're plumbline Christians." I could tell she wasn't satisfied with my attempt at a response as she eased away. I suspect what she really wanted to know was where I stand on social matters. A plumbline Christian would be one who condemns homosexuality, abortion under any circumstances, and the ordination of women, to name a few of the hotter issues.

The idea of the plumbline comes from Amos 7:7-9. Through Amos, God announces the destruction of Israel: "Look, I am going to measure my people Israel by a plumbline; no longer will I overlook their offenses. The high places of Isaac are going to be ruined, the sanctuaries of Israel destroyed, and, sword in hand, I will attack the House of Jeroboam."

A plumbline Christian must therefore be one who seeks to be obedient to God so that destruction will not be forthcoming. It is one who "toes the line" and rests assured of God's satisfaction.

Actually, "Plumbline Christian" is an oxymoron. Fastidious obedience to the laws of God for fear of God has nothing to do with Christian faith. Faith is not trusting in our obedience to the law, but in the Grace of God. Faith is knowing that we have all sinned and that none of us can claim to be aligned properly. Faith is not separating ourselves apart from the crowd in moral superiority, but rather immersing ourselves in the crowd as recipients of Christ's love, and in turn offering that love to others because we identify with them and feel compassion for them.

Speaking of plumblines, when did the church cross the line from being a welcoming sanctuary for those seeking forgiveness, acceptance and new life, and become a bastion of fear and prejudice toward others? When did we cross the line from being a cool cup of water to a thirsty world and become a fortress of protection from the evils of the world? When did we lose our vision for the future, knowing that the best is yet to come, and begin to cling desperately to "traditional values?" When did we stop trusting? When did our hearts grow hard?

These are sobering questions Christians need to ask of themselves and their churches. There is no place in the church for condemnation of others and self-righteousness. Obedience to the law is important, but we do so because we love God, not because we fear God. We are saved by God's love for us, not by our obedience. And when we live successfully in God's love we will by the nature of that love be obedient to God.

My visitor was, apparently, thinking that she is living according to God's plumbline because of her viewpoints, whatever they are. But when you think about it, she was not acting in love toward me. Did she meet me wherever I was coming from and seek to get to know me better? Did she honor me as a human being, a child of God? No, it was immediately apparent that there were strings upon her acceptance of me. Only if I were a plumbline Christian would I be a potential new friend.

If Christians treat one another this way, how do we treat everyone else?

My pastor says that "pluralism" is destroying the church. Is it wrong to believe that religions other than Christianity speak God's truth, too?

God speaks through all religions. God even speaks through the secular world. After all, everything is created by God. Pluralism is threatening to those who feel they have the absolute truth. But because of our inability to grasp truth fully, we must be open to learning from one another. Personally, I think pluralism has always been the saving grace of the Judeo-Christian tradition.

In the Hebrew scriptures, we see an evolving struggle between desire for purity in the faith and the need for tolerance of other cultures. The Wisdom literature, in particular, largely favors openness and dialogue. The books of Ruth and Jonah, for example, teach us that God's favor is not extended only to the so-called people of the covenant. Rather, the covenant people are enriched by tolerance and fellowship with those who are different from themselves. The faithfulness of Ruth, who was not a Hebrew woman, contributed to the bloodline of King David, and eventually, Jesus.

Further, the covenant people were sometimes restored to wholeness by one who was not of their own culture, as when God used Cyrus, the King of Persia, to return the people to their Promised Land. These historical blessings of pluralism ran counter to efforts of some religious leaders in Hebrew history to purge the people of all "impurities," as in the time of Ezra and Nehemiah.

In the Greek scriptures (the New Testament), Jesus confronts the efforts of religious leaders to purify their faith. His ministry is inclusive and affirming of all people. It transcends religious traditions and conventional doctrine in order to invite people to a meaningful relationship with God, the creator of all. The belief that Jesus died for all people is a strong case for pluralistic participation in the Kingdom of God.

The Bible reveals that the early church had its own struggles with pluralism. What made the church what it is supposed to be today - embracing all people unconditionally with faith alone - was hammered out of controversy between St. Peter and St. Paul over the inclusion of Gentiles within Christianity.

Christian tradition after the Bible was canonized contains similar struggles between those who wish to purge the church of "outside" influences and those who value pluralism. The Reformation itself might be seen in the light of the spirit moving to protect pluralism in the face of dogmatism, exploitation and manipulation. The argument still rages as to whether or not Protestants belong to the true church, yet one wonders where Christianity would be without the rich fabric of these "heretics."

I must also say, however, that pluralism is not good simply for its own sake. Not everything that a religion says (including Christianity), or everything in the secular world, is God's truth. God's ways are not our ways, so the prophet Isaiah tells us. We have a duty, therefore, as people of faith, to try to align ourselves with God's ways discerned with our tradition and to work toward the reform of those ideas formulated from selfish, fearful or biases motives.

Pluralism does not mean "anything goes." Nor does it mean that what we say or do makes no difference. That's not pluralism. That's foolishness. People of faith can come to understand their traditions to contain truth yet not consider those to be the only containers. We can be open to truth received in a pluralistic way, while standing up against what violates the love of God. We can affirm the goodness we see in all religions and give thanks to God for it.

Does pluralism mean betraying Jesus? On the contrary, I think it is the only way to be true to Jesus.

I'm happy to see all of the interest in preserving the Earth, but as a Christian, I'm uncomfortable participating in Earth Day. It seems to be a gathering of Goddess worshipers, secular humanists and pagan cults. How do you feel about a Christian participating in Earth Day celebrations?

Christians often feel compromised in situations where something worthwhile is happening in the community, but where Jesus is not honored as Lord and Savior. Earth Day is certainly one of those times. Other occasions might be a school graduation, or an inter-faith Thanksgiving Day service, or perhaps a wedding ceremony where the bride and groom are not particularly religious.

We should never fear entering into secular or even anti-Christian situations. Where else are we going to rub shoulders with people who don't know Jesus? Furthermore, we become a lot less judgmental of others by having firsthand experiences of them.

We find, perhaps, that there are many common values between what Jesus teaches us and what other people believe. We find bridges over which to communicate and build up the whole community. Also, we find that our own faith can grow by the ideas of others, even when they are not Christian.

Earth Day is an example of important ideas which the Christian faith has largely neglected over the centuries. Christian theology certainly contains a basis for valuing the Earth and nurturing it, but Earth-centered thinking has traditionally been identified with paganism.

Missionary practices have often denigrated the spiritual values which Earth-centered cultures enjoyed and could have offered back to Christianity. In our efforts to bring the world to Christ, we can destroy what Christ might have to say to us through others' beliefs and cultures.

Modern missionary efforts tend in many cases to honor local

culture and to incorporate indigenous values into their Christian proclamation.

Western ideas are largely hostile to Earth-centered ways of being, however, and Western Christian faith is the child of a "conquering the world" mentality. This is why Earth Day is good for Christians.

Matthew Fox, one of the contemporary Christian leaders in creation-affirming Christian theology, sets forth some of the contrasts between traditional Christian attitudes toward creation and earth-centered attitudes. You can find this in a good little book called <u>On becoming a Musical Mystical Bear.</u>

Fox says Christianity has been dominated by Greek philosophical ideas, which reduce the material world to something less than spiritual, while, in Hebrew thinking, spiritual means that which is life-giving. Rather than the soul struggling with the demands of the Spirit and the temptations of the world, we ought to be struggling as whole persons with evil in its many forms.

Christianity has largely condemned the pleasures of the world as sinful, at most to be limited, while Hebrew tradition views material things as God-made and holy, to be enjoyed as a gift from the creator.

Christian dogma traditionally centers around the theological theme of the fall and humankind's need for redemption. Earth-centered Christian theology centers on the goodness of creation and saying thank you to God by enjoying our blessings, sharing them with the less fortunate, and taking care of creation.

Stewardship has often been reduced to fund raising for the church institution rather than cultivating an awareness of the trust which has been charged to us by God for the protection of our environment which not only sustains us, but is also the work of our creator and worthy of protection for its own glory.

Christians might recognize the significance of Earth Day as a friend of the firstborn of all creation and give thanks for the values it promotes. These are Christian values, too.

*There is a pastor of the
Dutch Reformed Churdh of America serving in my state
of Michigan who is creating quite a stir with his belief
that Jesus is not the only way to God. Is this what you
believe as well?*

I don't know the specifics of this pastor's beliefs, but I would be happy to share my own.

Jesus is considered by Christians to be the only way of salvation. This does not lead to the conclusion, however, that one must be a Christian to be acceptable to God. Nor does it mean that only Christians are going to receive entrance into heaven. If Jesus is God, as we Christians believe, then we should know that God finds all people acceptable from Jesus' own teaching.

Jesus addressed the issue while walking with his disciples. James and John said to him, "Teacher...Grant us to sit, one at your right hand and one at your left, in your glory." Jesus' response should be remembered by those who assume the their discipleship affords them special privileges. "You do not know what you are asking. Are you able to drink the cup that I will drink, or be baptized with the baptism that I am baptized with?... To sit at my right hand or my left is not mine to grant, but it is for those for whom it has been prepared."

Jesus is the only way because he reveals to us that there is no one human way to God. Our entrance into the Kingdom of God, indeed our ability to even relate to God, is a gift to us. Tradition calls it grace, or unconditional love.

The inclusiveness of Christianity is not based upon the idea that all world religions have value, which of course they do, or that one path is as good as another, which of course, it may not be. Rather, it is based on Jesus himself. The Incarnation states that God has come - and comes - to us where we are. It is God's action, not ours, which saves us.

God looks upon all human beings as beloved children, and will not rest until all who wish to be are present at the table.

Exactly how this universal understanding of salvation will play out we cannot know. But because of Jesus we know its essential ingredients: God sees us all as equals, finds us when we are lost, invites us to the banquet, gives us the freedom to say no, and if we say yes, commands us to serve.

By the way, "we" includes everyone. Christians are called to deliver that message because reconciliation with God enlivens human beings and bears the fruit of God's spirit in human relationships. But if we fail out of human limitation, ignorance, or our own sinfulness, we can trust that God will ultimately find a way to deliver it in spite of us.

Tragically, the James and John syndrome has dominated the mission of the church througout history and is very much alive today. Christians need to remember that Jesus was crucified because of it. He was rejected by the religious leaders of his own day, and abandoned by his own disciples, not becuse he failed to confront the evils they faced in the world around them, but because he confronted the evil within themselves. He was killed not because he was a failure, but because he was a threat to the exclusiveness of his religious community.

Jesus was rejected because of his inclusive teaching and behavior, demonstrated in almost every Gospel story. His way is the only way because it invites us to dissolve the human divisions we create out of fear of those not like ourselves, to appreciate the sacred dignity of every human being, and to work together to manifest the diverse gifts which God has bestowed upon humanity.

When we see these qualities in any human being, we are looking upon the face of Christ. It is simply God's way, and whatever we call ourselves, we either follow it or we don't.

> *I sometimes find myself in situations where I am asked to pray in the company of both Christians and non-Christians. I want to pray in the name of Jesus Christ, but I do not want to disregard the presence of non-Christians. What would you suggest in such situations?*

Your struggle over this matter reflects a loving sensitivity to others. I congratulate you on having the courage to question a sacrosanct Christian tradition which has led to arrogance on the part of Christians and therefore impaired their witness for Christ's love.

Two biblical passages come to mind. Jesus says in John 15:7, "If you abide I me, and my words abide in you, ask for whatever you wish, and it will be done for you." And in Colossians 3:17 Paul says, "Whatever you do, in word or deed, do everything in the name of the Lord Jesus, giving thanks to God the Father through him." Both of these passages invite the reader to trust that Jesus is the bearer of God's grace to humanity and that we an be thankful in all things because of Jesus. They are statements intended to express the unconditional love of God, not to give Christians a tool with which to diminish non-Christians.

To pray in the name of Jesus is often wrongly understood as a magical incantation. It is not a formula which opens the ears of God. Rather, it is to pray with faith in Jesus. It is to place our prayer in the context of an understanding of God derived from a relationship with Jesus as the one who gave his life for the salvation of the world. To pray in the name of Jesus is to desire the heart of Jesus.

Christians are called, first and foremost, to do what is loving. It is important to remember that everything we do is in the name of Jesus. We are witnesses to what it is to be a Christian whether we are doing something intentional, such as a public prayer, or whether we are "off duty" shopping at the grocery store. We put a face on Jesus to the world and we honor or dishonor his name with every word and deed. The impression we make upon others is the impression they will have, in part, of what it is to be a Christian.

Certainly when among Christians it is appropriate to use the words, "in the name of Jesus." This holds up before us the essential connections between Jesus and our understanding of God. In a mixed crowd, however, such a formula can defeat our loving witness for Christ to others. It disregards their presence and gives the message that in God's eyes they are out of favor. There is a better way.

One must ask, "What can I do to best show forth the love of Christ for every person present?" The answer to this question will depend upon the circumstances. I was once invited to pray at a breakfast to honor volunteers for the Salvation Army. Being a Christian organization, a prayer in the name of Christ would certainly be appropriate. But gathered in the room were many from the community who were not Christian. I was aware, for example, of the presence of several friends from the local synagogue. I prefaced my Christian prayer by noting that not everyone in the room is Christian, yet we are gathered to honor a loving work of the whole community through a Christian organization. My Christian prayer should be understood, therefore, to express the unconditional love of God for all human beings, which is what Jesus teaches us.

After the breakfast one of the Jewish women thanked me for saying a prayer in which she felt she could participate fully, even though it was a Christian prayer. I believe I served Christ better than if I had ignored her presence.

Other circumstances may call for a different approach. It is far more difficult to abide in Christ than it is to simply speak in the name of Christ. It requires sensitivity to the setting and prayerful preparation. I encourage you not to be dogmatic and allow the Holy Spirit to guide you to say what is most loving as you lead people in prayer.

Christians are known by the fruit they bear, not by the formulas they use.

TOPICAL INDEX

INDEX

INDEX

BIBILICAL INDEX

INDEX

243

FRIENDS IN FAITH

Mail Order Information:

For additional copies of *Friends in Faith* send $14.95 per book plus $1.50 for shipping and handling. California residents add 7.25% sales tax. Make checks payable to FIF, P.O. Box 1296, Carmel, California 93921 Telephone (408) 624-3883.

Also available through local bookstores that use R.R. Bowker Company *BOOKS IN PRINT* catalogue system. Order through publisher SUNFLOWER INK PUBLISHING, 37931 Palo Colorado Road, Carmel, CA 93923 for bookstore discount. Telephone: (408) 625-0588 Fax: (408) 625-3770